VGM Opportunities Series

OPPORTUNITIES IN
ADVERTISING
CAREERS

S. William Pattis

Revised by
Jeff Johnson

Foreword by
Ruth Wooden
President
The Advertising Council

 **VGM Career Horizons**
a division of *NTC Publishing Group*
Lincolnwood, Illinois USA

Cover Photo Credits:

Lower left: Leo Burnett USA; all other photographs courtesy of BBDO Chicago.

Library of Congress Cataloging–in–Publication Data

Pattis, S. William
    Opportunities in advertising careers / S. William Pattis ; revised
by Jeff Johnson ; foreword by Ruth Wooden.
        p.   cm.
    Includes bibliographical references.
    ISBN 0–8442–4442–2 (hard). — ISBN 0–8442–4443–0 (soft)
    1. Rev. ed. of: Advertising : a VGM career planner.
    2. Advertising—Vocational guidance.   3. Advertising—United States
—Vocational guidance.   4. Advertising—United States—Information
services.   I. Johnson, Jeff, 1956–   .   II. Pattis, S. William.
Advertising.   III. Title.
HF5827.P38   1995
659.1'023'73—dc20   94–49545
                                                                                    CIP

Published by VGM Career Horizons, a division of NTC Publishing Group
4255 West Touhy Avenue
Lincolnwood (Chicago), Illinois 60646-1975, U.S.A.

5 6 7 8 9 0 VP 9 8 7 6 5 4 3 2 1

9S(8(2

CONTENTS

ABOUT THE AUTHOR

S. William "Bill" Pattis started his lifetime career in publishing and advertising in 1933, when at the age of eight he sold the *Saturday Evening Post* for a nickel a copy to commuters at the neighborhood train station in Chicago's Hyde Park community. At twelve, he was a co-owner of a corner newsstand.

His career came to a standstill for the next nine years as he finished high school, served in Europe as a combat engineer during World War II, and completed his studies obtaining a degree in marketing and management at the University of Illinois in 1949. While in college, he was heavily involved in extracurricular activities that contributed much to his flair for advertising and promotion.

His first postcollege job was in Chicago selling advertising for United Business Publications at $40 per week. He progressed rapidly and at age twenty-nine was moved to New York by his employer to become publisher of *Photographic Trade News.* In quick succession, his responsibilities were expanded to assume the full publishing responsibilities for five business magazines.

At thirty-three, he returned to Chicago to establish The Pattis Group, which he ran for almost thirty years. The firm became the world's largest in magazine advertising sales, with nine offices in the United States and abroad. The Pattis Group dealt on a daily basis with most national advertisers and probably all of the advertising agencies in America; the scope of these activities has formed the basis for much of the knowledge and information found in this book. In 1988, the firm was sold to the 3M company and became known as 3M/Pattis.

The author's writings include many articles that have appeared in the advertising press, including periodicals such as *Folio, Mediascope, Media Form, The American Business Press* publication, *Sales Talk,* and others. His speaking engagements have included appearances before The National Association of Publishers Representatives, The Overseas Press and Media Association, and the International Media Buyers' Association. He participated in the first Face-to-Face International conference in The Hague, Netherlands, and has been a principal speaker at the annual meeting of the Periodical Publishers Association of the United Kingdom.

As is typical for many people in communications, he has served on various civic and charitable committees throughout his business life. In the late 1960s and early 1970s, he received commendations from both Vice-Presidents Humphrey and Agnew for his work on the President's Council for Youth Opportunity. Presently he serves on the Book and Library Committee of the United States Information Agency and is on the Executive Committee of the Publishing Hall of Fame. During the Bush administration, he served for four years as the Chairman of the Book & Library Advisory Committee of the U.S. Information Agency.

Revision assistance was provided by Jeff Johnson, a freelance writer and editor who has written and collaborated on a number of career books for young people. Jeff

is a Phi Beta Kappa graduate of Northwestern University
and is in the midst of a budding career with Warner Bros.
Records. As a recording artist and songwriter, he has re-
leased two Top 10 dance hits on the Interhit label.

FOREWORD

Advertising is an often maligned industry—one whose value to society is frequently questioned or misunderstood. The benefits of advertising are often overlooked. Advertising helps to encourage competitive pricing and product innovation. It helps to support the media, and it subsidizes news, as well as cultural and sporting events. But most importantly, advertising provides consumers with information to make sound choices.

I enjoyed the early part of my career as an agency account executive for some major commercial products. However, the work I found most rewarding was overseeing a pro-bono campaign offering help to teenage alcoholics. It was then that I discovered the tremendous power of advertising as a tool to communicate life-saving information.

It is amazing to consider some of public service advertising's greatest success stories. One of our first campaigns during World War II resulted in 85 million Americans purchasing war bonds. More recently, our drunk driving prevention and safety belt campaigns have helped to reduce highway fatalities to the lowest level in 30 years. And our campaign to recruit teachers has resulted in over 800,000 phone calls to our hotline. More than 40,000 of those callers are now teachers. All of this and much more was brought about by thousands of advertisers and advertising agencies volunteering their time and talents.

If you choose a career in advertising, please remember that it gives you more than the opportunity to sell products and services. It gives you the power to prevent disease, accidents, and abuse—the power to make the world in which we live a safer and healthier place.

Ruth A. Wooden
President, The Advertising Council

PREFACE

Writing a career book about a business in which you have spent your entire adult life is a mix of pleasure and frustration. The enjoyment is in looking back and recalling personal accomplishments, friendships, and other pleasant experiences. The frustration is recognizing that all of this has to be translated to the "here and now" and reminding myself that the reader is on the outside and wanting in.

Assembling a book like this calls for the cooperation of many people. Additional information has been gathered from the advertising press and friends in the advertising business. I also am grateful to the estate of Harry Groome for granting permission to use material on the history of advertising from an earlier work authored by Mr. Groome.

A special thanks to my wife Bette, son Mark, and daughter Robin for tolerating the talk about advertising and publishing that dominated our earlier years for better or for worse. The advertising and publishing business has been fun, it has been stimulating, and I have many fond memories. It is now time for the next generation.

The world of advertising is an exciting environment that breeds great rewards, both personal and financial. It is not a business for people who seek a tranquil existence. If, after reading this book, you believe you have the personal characteristics coupled with the drive, ambition, and competitiveness to be a success, you should take the plunge and get that first job. If you do well, the rest will follow.

S. William Pattis

INTRODUCTION

Advertising is so pervasive in our society today that unless you are a hermit, you probably see literally dozens of advertisements every day. And even if you *are* a hermit, there is a good chance you may have found your cave through an ad. Most people think of advertising in terms of television commercials, magazine ads, or retail ads printed in the Sunday paper, but advertising encompasses a much wider range of skills, services, and media. The campaign poster for the upcoming mayoral race, the little heart that the neighbor soliciting for the Heart Fund gives you, and the window displays in the downtown department stores are all forms of advertising. In the United States, advertising is a vital and major contributor to the growth of our national economy.

To create the many types of advertising that surround us requires the work of many people with a wide variety of skills. In all probability, the thirty-second commercial that interrupted your favorite TV show last night represented the work of advertising agency creative people, artists, writers, film crews, directors, models, makeup artists, and dozens of other people. Many of these people work for one of the United States' 6,000 advertising agencies or the many specialized firms that provide these services. These people possess diverse abilities, ranging from business knowledge to the ability to write and illustrate appealing advertisements, and yet each performs a needed task in bringing the final message to you.

In this book we will try to describe some of the many positions that can be found in the advertising profession and help you understand the kind of work that each advertising professional performs. In addition to covering the advertising agency business, we will explore other ways that advertising skills can be employed. Last, but certainly not least, we will consider some of the educational and practical preparation you may need to land your first job in advertising—a job that, if you possess the creativity, determination, and maturity needed, will be your first step in a successful career in the advertising industry.

CHAPTER 1

ADVERTISING—THEN AND NOW

Wherever you go, whatever you do in today's world, you cannot escape advertising. It has become a part of almost every culture in some way. You can't travel to any city in the world without encountering advertising in one form or another. It's importance cannot be overlooked, simply because it helps to inform the public of the basic goods and services that are available in the marketplace. Advertisers reach the public through a variety of ways, including radio, television, newspapers, magazines, direct mail, billboards, posters, catalogs, and brochures. Whenever you turn on the television, pick up a magazine, or drive down the highway, you encounter advertising, and advertisers will use as many different forms of advertising as is economically feasible in order to reach the greatest number of people. Whether they are promoting a product, service, or idea, advertisers are in the business of selling.

The word advertising comes from the French verb *advertir* meaning "to warn, call attention to." The American Marketing Association offers this definition: "the paid, nonpersonal presentation of goods, services and ideas by an identified sponsor." The key word here is *paid.* This is the difference between advertising and publicity. Manufacturers usually have to pay for the promotion of their products, services, or ideas. Publicity can be thought of as free advertising. When products or services are mentioned in a positive way on television or radio or in newspapers or magazines, this is publicity. Publicity spreads the word about a product or service and is purely informational or simply entertaining for the audience, but it is purely a voluntary occurrence on the part of the newspaper, radio station, or other communications vehicle. In the case of publicity, an advertiser has not paid for specific time or space to promote the product or service. We can see that "paid" is an important part of the definition of advertising.

Looking deeper at the AMA definition of advertising helps us to gain a better understanding of advertising. The term *nonpersonal* tells us that the message is intended to reach a large group of people, rather than a specific person. Advertising is not personal, one-to-one selling, but is accomplished through mass media, television, newspapers. The phrase *goods, services and ideas* shows that advertising covers a wide range of consumer needs. Advertising promotes not only products or goods, but also services, such as are offered by dry cleaners, banks, restaurants, those that repair appliances, and so forth. Besides services, ideas are being increasingly promoted through advertising. One look at the amount of paid political advertising during an election campaign tells us the importance of advertising in furthering ideas. The politician uses advertising to influence voters into accepting his or her political ideas and in turn supporting his or her quest for political office. Television advertising has become the fastest way to reach the greatest number of voters and has, unfortunately, led to an unprecedented amount of negative advertising and personal attacks by candidates. As we can see, advertising is far more complex than simply selling a can of soup. Continuing with our definition, *an identified sponsor* allows the viewer or reader of the advertisement to identify the producer of the product, the company offering the service, or the group promoting the idea. If we don't know who is selling the product or service, we don't know what to ask for or where to go to get it. Often advertising tells us the brand name of the product, so we then are able to identify the product with the producer. It obviously would be pointless to advertise without indicating the sponsor and brand name.

Besides placing ads in the various forms of media, advertisers can also employ consumer promotions, trade promotions, and point-of-purchase advertising. Consumer promotions include coupons, special sales, contests, or any type of special offering that attempts to persuade the consumer to purchase a product or service. Trade promotions consist of special offers made to wholesalers and retailers, such as "buy one thousand units and get one hundred free" or "order before this date and receive no bill until a later date." Exhibits and trade shows also fall under the umbrella of trade promotions. Point-of-purchase advertising, as one might think, occurs at the point where the product is made available for sale. This type of advertising can include unique product displays such as banners, posters, and neon signs. Point-of-purchase advertising draws attention to the product right where the consumer is—in the supermarket, department store, or hardware store, for example. It often has a great effect because it can make a product stand out from the other products, and the consumer can purchase the product right then and there, as opposed to seeing it on TV and having to make the trip to find the product. The immediacy of point-of-purchase advertising makes it a powerful tool for the advertiser.

Advertising provides a connection between someone offering something and someone needing something. The advertiser provides information to those seeking it, informs the public of what's available, and tells them how to get it. It is the most effective way of reaching the consumer. Most media depend on advertising for most or all of their revenues. One may forget that most television and radio programs are funded through advertising revenue. Also, most newspapers and magazines depend on advertising to absorb their costs and to help to generate profits. Without advertising there would be little need for billboards, posters, and catalogs. Advertising's importance to the communications industry is immeasurable. In fact, most of the media we take for granted would be extremely expensive to the viewer or reader without the income produced by advertising. Advertising dollars truly keep our media thriving.

Advertising agencies play a crucial role in today's advertising business. These agencies are responsible for creating, producing, and placing ads for their clients. Advertising agencies may also provide assistance in other areas, such as sales and marketing, public relations, and market research. Agency size can range from a few people to thousands, but within each agency, large or small, one or more people handle the different functions needed to produce the ads and to see that they appear in the right place at the right time. The most appealing job opportunities in the advertising business for young people are found within the advertising agency.

A career in advertising can be rewarding and exciting. Though, after years of remarkable growth, the industry suffered a recent downturn, this should not discourage those interested in this profession. A recovery appears to be underway, and a leaner more effective workforce should help the industry to thrive as it enters the next century.

HISTORY OF ADVERTISING

Taking a look at the history of advertising through the ages helps us to understand how advertising has grown to it's present level of influence and importance. Advertising, in one form or another, has been going on since ancient times. Even though early advertising was simple compared to today's standards, the basic reason for advertising was the same then as it is now—to communicate information about products, services, and ideas to groups of people.

The early craftsmen were among the world's first advertisers. In order to identify their work, they would place individual marks, or *trademarks,* on their goods. Similar to the brand names that we look for today while shopping for merchandise, these trademarks indicated to ancient buyers which craftsman created a particular object. As the reputation of a particular craftsman increased, people would look for that craftsman's trademark when buying goods. The trademark's usefulness in the world of commerce has a long history. Even today it protects manufacturers from those who would pass off inferior products under that manufacturer's name, and it protects the consumer by ensuring that they purchase the products that they desire.

Signs employed by tradespeople to state the nature of their business were found in the ruins of Babylon. Since few people could read, these signs showed pictures of the product or service for sale: a loaf of bread for a bakery, a boot for a shoemaker's shop. Excavations at Pompeii reveal a similar use of signs to indicate the type of shop and what it offered for sale. In ancient Egypt, items for sale and messages of interest were carved into stone tablets called *stelae* and placed on roads for the passersby to read. These tablets represented the first billboards—the precursors to today's billboards that one frequently finds along streets and highways.

In ancient Greece, men were paid to walk the streets telling the citizens of new and public events. These men were known as *town criers*. In Egypt, town criers told of the arrival of new merchandise on ships. As we can see, the spoken work played a role in advertising long before the advent of radio and television.

The Chinese invention of movable printing made printed handbills possible. Handbills were the earliest printed advertisements and were often bound into books. A handbill would usually show the sign that hung over the door of a particular shop and include brief copy underneath in script. The invention of the printing press in 1450 helped handbills evolve into the first newspapers. Almost as soon as the presses were rolling, they were being used for advertising. By the middle of the seventeenth century, weekly newspapers began to appear in England, and soon the British became the world leaders in advertising. Newspapers enticed businesses into advertising their products for sale on a grander scale. The most frequent early newspaper advertisers were importers of products new to the British Isles. For example, when coffee first became available in England in 1652, the announcement appeared in a newspaper ad. The first appearance of competitive advertising, as opposed to the simple announcement of new products being made available to the public, occurred in the early eighteenth century. In 1710 patent medicine advertisements appeared; these attempted to persuade readers that one product was better than another, similar, product. This type of advertising is extremely common today, though many of the claims made in these early ads may seem incredible and exaggerated to us.

A tax imposed by the Crown on both British newspapers and their advertisements severely curtailed the expansion of the advertising industry in England. In fact this tax represented one of the grievances the American colonists held against the British government during the time of the American Revolution. After the Revolution, the United States soon surpassed Britain to become the world leader in advertising.

The expansion of advertising's influence in society occurred in earnest in the mid-nineteenth century with the invention of the steam engine and the advent of the Industrial Revolution. The Civil War created the need for mass production, and as the country grew, so did the need for factory-made goods. At the same time manufacturers needed to spread the word about their products to an ever-expanding consumer base and consequently turned to advertising to do the job. By communicating the availability of products to more people, sales increased, thus allowing manufacturers to produce more and consequently charge less for their products. In this way advertising helped to fuel the Industrial Revolution. Another important element in the expanding economy of the nineteenth century was transportation. Without an efficient and all-encompassing transportation system, goods cannot get to the markets where they are needed. In the United States, the railroad provided the system whereby these goods made it around the country. By the 1890s the entire country had been connected together by railroads, which helped the country to become a more unified market, rather than a group of local and regional markets. Other technological innovations helped to fuel the remarkable growth of the advertising industry in the late nineteenth century. These included the invention of the rotary press in 1849, the manufacture of paper from wood pulp in 1866, the arrival of the linotype in 1884, and the invention of halftone engraving in 1893.

As the economy grew, so did the number of newspapers and magazines and thus the number of ads placed. In 1830 there were 1,200 U.S. newspapers. By 1860 there were about 3,000. The peak was reached in 1914 when there were 15,000 newspapers in circulation in this country. In 1850 there were approximately 700 magazines in the United States, and by 1880 this number had grown to 2,400. By 1900 it had doubled to 4,800. As the number of magazines and newspapers increased, advertising became more and more prevalent than ever before.

Up until the middle of the nineteenth century, merchants wrote and placed their own advertising in local magazines and newspapers. With the Industrial Revolution, many businesses were eager to expand their sales into broader markets. Soon publishers of newspapers and magazines hired advertising agents to help to sell advertising to retailers and manufacturers. These agents acted as liaisons between the publisher and the advertiser, and the ads were usually prepared by the advertiser or the advertising agent. Basically these advertising agents served as the first advertising agencies. Generally agents were hired by the publishers, not the advertisers. Other so-called agents were simply brokers of space. They would negotiate to buy space in a newspaper or magazine at a good rate and then sell this space to the advertiser for a higher rate in order to make a profit. As a result of this practice, advertising agents gained bad reputations.

In the late 1860s N. W. Ayer helped change this negative perception of the advertising business by instituting a major shift in the focus of the entire advertising system. Ayer believed that it would be better to represent the interests of the advertisers rather than those of the publishers. As a consequence of this belief, Ayer started the first advertising agency and based it on this concept. He hired writers and artists and persuaded the advertisers that his company could actually create the advertising and, with the support of his agency, achieve better results. N. W. Ayer not only brought organization and order to the advertising business, he also gave it a much needed boost in credibility. At the beginning of the twentieth century, advertising agencies had taken the role that they fill today, including the creation, organization, and execution of advertising campaigns for their clients.

With the twentieth century came a communications revolution that fueled unprecedented growth in the advertising industry. Radio and television brought the advertiser's message to millions instantly. No longer did advertisers have to rely on the printed word to get their message across. Even those who could not read could be reached through these new mass communications tools. Marconi transmitted the first wireless message in 1895. By 1922 there were thirty radio stations licensed by the Federal Communications Commission (FCC). In 1926 NBC became the first broadcasting company to air the same program all over the country. In the 1930s and 1940s, the radio industry experienced great growth and became a formidable influence in people's lives. It was also during this period that the practice of using popular celebrities to endorse products first became common. Today celebrity endorsements often play a vital role in the success of a product. Commercial radio made it possible for national advertisers to reach large numbers of people and to expand their coverage of the market. Many products sponsored entire shows, such as the Texaco Star Theater and the Jello Program, which garnered large, devoted audiences. By associating a product with a popular radio show, both the company's image and sales benefited. Today there are more than 9,500 radio stations in the United States alone, and advertisers spend close to $9 billion a year on radio advertising.

Television's arrival on the scene in the 1950s signaled the end of radio's dominance and the beginning of another boom in the advertising industry. The ability to reach millions of households with a visual image led to further growth for the advertising industry. Television sets were the fastest selling appliances in the 1950s, and this signaled the beginning of the transfer of advertising dollars from radio and print media to television. Advertisers who had been using only words and still pictures to sell their products now combined sight, sound, *and* motion to their message. By 1955 advertisers were spending over $1 billion a year on television advertising. Today this figure amounts to over $30 billion. To illustrate the power of TV advertising, a thirty-second commercial on prime time TV may be seen by 100 million people or more at the same time. As advertisers have discovered, the effect that advertising on television has on sales is staggering. In recent years, cable television has added another lucrative dimension to television advertising. Like prime time TV, cable airs conventional commercials, but certain cable stations, like QVC and The Home Shopping Network, allow viewers to actually buy the products they see on TV from the comfort of their own homes. Others offer half-hour or hour-long paid commercials called Infomercials. With a modem and computer, even small companies can advertise and sell their products to the rapidly growing community of "on-line" home computer users. Also, with the coming five-hundred-channel cable set-up, interactive TV, and the birth of the "Information Superhighway," advertising is set to enter another period of possible great growth and innovation. As communication has advanced, so has advertising continued to advance and to provide new and exciting ways to inform people about products and services.

ADVERTISING AND THE ECONOMY

A cause for great debate in the advertising industry is the question of advertising's effect and influence on the economy. Some argue that advertising makes a great contribution to the economy, while others attempt to downplay advertising's role in this area. It is obvious from the sheer volume of dollars spent on advertising every year, coupled with the fact that advertising sells products and services, that advertising does have an undeniable influence on the economy. Measuring that influence is another story. Advertising plays an important role in the distribution of goods and services, and the demand created by advertising helps the economy to expand by stimulating demand for particular products and services. Obviously the cost of advertising is included in the cost of the product or service, but those who advertise know that advertising translates into sales and that prices can be reduced through the increased production caused by increased demand. Advertising can truly mean the difference between success and failure for the manufacturer. As much as one-third of the total sales and manufacturing and marketing expenses of certain low-cost, frequently purchased products is spent on advertising. This highlights the importance that certain companies attach to advertising. Companies rely so strongly on advertising simply because it sells their products. This is all the proof these manufacturers need of the influence of advertising on the economy.

It should be noted that advertising's economic influence varies widely from product to product. Advertising contributes most to the sales of products like cosmetics, medicines, cereals, candy bars, and other packaged goods. Advertising plays a lesser role in the sales of products like industrial equipment or boats, for example. Goods and services that are sold by mail order depend exclusively on advertising, because it is the only way for buyers to learn how and where to purchase these goods and services.

If advertising influences the economy, it is also clear that the economy influences advertising. The recessions of 1980–1981 and 1990–1992 had a great impact on the advertising industry. These economic downturns led to decreases in billings and layoffs within the industry, proving that the same industry that helps to fuel the economy suffers when the economy takes a turn for the worse.

ADVERTISING CODES AND REGULATIONS

The government protects the public from fraudulent and misleading advertising through various laws, codes, regulations, and principles. The amount of misleading or false advertising has decreased in recent years due to these restrictions. In the United States, the Federal Trade Commission (FTC) monitors advertising in order to decide whether it is false or misleading. The FTC may require advertisers to provide proof of their claims or may order advertisers to remove ads that are considered questionable. Specific types of advertising are regulated by other government agencies.

Though these agencies are concerned with the public welfare and believe that they know what is "right," advertisers often have their own concept of what is "right" and disagree with the judgments of these agencies. Perhaps a reasonable consensus can be reached someday, but until then, advertisers and government agencies may continue to be at odds on certain issues.

The advertising industry's concern with maintaining respectability and truth in advertising has led to the establishment of several voluntary associations that operate under self-imposed regulations designed to discourage and penalize improper or unethical practices. These include the American Association of Advertising Agencies; the Association of National Advertisers; the National Association of Broadcasters, which regulates what airs on television and radio; and the Magazine Publishers Association and the American Association of Business Publishers, which monitor the advertising content of magazines.

The National Advertising Division (NAD), formed by agencies and advertisers along with the National Better Business Bureau, reviews complaints about misleading or false advertising. The NAD goes as far as to investigate complaints and to make efforts to arrange settlements between the parties involved. If no settlement can be reached, an appeal can be made to the National Advertising Review Board, a five-member body with representatives from advertising and the public sector. This board has the power to pull or change advertising that it considers questionable.

Despite the often commendable efforts of these regulatory groups, abuses and false advertising claims still occur, though less and less frequently. One could say that some of today's advertising is considered objectionable due to poor taste rather than to any actual fraudulence. Since taste is subjective, it seems probable that this situation will continue. No uniform standards of tastes appear likely in the future.

The self-imposed code of the American Advertising Federation reads as follows:

The Advertising Code of American Business

1. *Truth* . . . Advertising shall tell the truth, and shall reveal significant facts, the concealment of which would mislead the public.
2. *Responsibility* . . . Advertising agencies and advertisers shall be willing to provide substantiation of claims made.
3. *Taste and Decency* . . . Advertising shall be free of statements, illustrations, or implications which are offensive to good taste or public decency.

4. *Bait Advertising* . . . Advertising shall offer only merchandise or services which are readily available for
purchase at the advertised price.
5. *Guarantees and Warranties* . . . Advertising of guarantees and warranties shall be explicit. Advertising of
any guarantee or warranty shall clearly and conspicu-
ously disclose its nature and extent, the manner in
which the guarantor or warrantor will perform, and
the identity of the guarantor or warrantor.
6. *Price Claims* . . . Advertising shall avoid price or savings claims which are false or misleading, or which
do not offer provable bargains or savings.
7. *Unprovable Claims* . . . Advertising shall avoid the
use of exaggerated or unprovable claims.
8. *Testimonials* . . . Advertising containing testimonials
shall be limited to those of competent witnesses who
are reflecting a real and honest choice.

Standards of Practice of the American Association of Advertising Agencies

*First adopted on October 16, 1924. Most recently re-
vised on September 18, 1990.*

We hold that a responsibility of advertising agencies is to be a constructive force in business.

We hold that, to discharge this responsibility, advertising agencies must recognize an obligation, not
only to their clients, but to the public, the media they
employ, and to each other. As a business, the advertising agency must operate within the framework of
competition. It is recognized that keen and vigorous

competition, honestly conducted, is necessary to the growth and the health of American business. However, unethical competitive practices in the advertising agency business lead to financial waste, dilution of service, diversion of manpower, loss of credibility, and tend to weaken public confidence both in advertisements and in the institution of advertising. The advertising agency should compete on merit and not by attempts at discrediting or disparaging a competitive agency, or its work.

To these ends, the American Association of Advertising Agencies has adopted the following *Creative Code* as being in the best interests of the public, the advertisers, the media, and the agencies themselves. The AAAA believes the Code's provisions serve as a guide to the kind of agency conduct that experience has shown to be wise, foresighted, and constructive. In accepting membership, and agency agrees to follow it.

Creative Code

We, the members of the American Association of Advertising Agencies, in addition to supporting and obeying the laws and legal regulations pertaining to advertising, undertake to extend and broaden the application of high ethical standards. Specifically, we will not knowingly create advertising that contains:

a. False or misleading statements of exaggerations, visual or verbal.

b. Testimonials that do not reflect the real opinion of the individual(s) involved.

c. Price claims that are misleading.

d. Claims insufficiently supported or that distort the true meaning or practicable application of statements made by professional or scientific authority.

e. Statements, suggestions, or pictures offensive to public decency or minority segments of the population.

We recognize that there are areas that are subject to honestly different interpretations and judgment. Nevertheless, we agree not to recommend to an advertiser, and to discourage the use of, advertising that is in poor or questionable taste or that is deliberately irritating through aural or visual content or presentation.

Comparative advertising shall be governed by the same standards of truthfulness, claim substantiation, tastefulness, etc., as apply to other types of advertising.

These Standards of Practice of the American Association of Advertising Agencies come from the belief that sound and ethical practice is good business. Confidence and respect are indispensable to success in a business embracing the many intangibles of agency service and involving relationships so dependent upon good faith.

Clear and willful violating of these Standards of Practice may be referred to the Board of Directors of the American Association of Advertising Agencies for appropriate action, including possible annulment of membership as provided by Article IV, Section 5, of the Constitution and By-Laws.[*]

---

[*]Copyright 1990 American Association of Advertising Agencies.

ADVERTISING AND PUBLIC CAUSES

One of the most important and influential organizations in the advertising industry is the Advertising Council. The Ad Council presents public service announcements (PSAs) and other forms of advertising dedicated to the improvement of society as a whole. The Ad Council coordinates advertisers, advertising agencies, and media in its efforts to create effective public service messages and to deliver those messages to the public. All creative time and effort and media are contributed for free for the general public welfare. In fact, one third of all PSAs are Ad Council campaigns. These campaigns also include programs targeted to specific minority communities. As an indication of the scope of the Ad Council's activities, estimated media dollar values would place the Ad Council among the country's top ten advertisers. The efforts of the Ad Council provide the advertising industry with a way to use its talents and resources to help people, and over the last fifty years, the work of the Ad Council has had an extremely positive effect in this country. Beginning with World War II campaigns like "A Slip of Lip Will Sink a Ship" through the well-known Smokey the Bear "Only You Can Prevent Forest Fires" and the United Negro College Fund's "A Mind is a Terrible Thing To Waste" campaigns, the Ad Council has left its mark in the public's thought. And the Ad Council continues its positive work today. For example, 1992 marked the first year since the 1940s that automobile fatalities dropped below forty thousand, an achievement for which the government gave considerable credit to the

Ad Council's "Buckle Up" and "Friends Don't Let Friends Drive Drunk" campaigns.
  Causes supported by the Advertising Council include:

Community Service
American Red Cross
Antidiscrimination
The Arts and Humanities
Breaking the Cycle of Disadvantage
Individual Giving and Volunteering
The Points of Light Foundation/Community Service

Education
Education Reform
Head Start
Junior Achievement
Recruiting New Teachers
United Negro College Fund
Value of Math and Science

Environment
Buy Recycled
Clean Water
Earth Share
Forest Fire Prevention

Health Concerns
American Red Cross Health and Safety
Breast Cancer Detection
Child Abuse Prevention
Infant Immunization
Healthy Start
Organ and Tissue Donation

Public Safety
Crime Prevention
Drunk Driving Prevention
Employer Support of the Guard and Reserve
For a Safer America
Safety Belt Education
Substance Abuse
Drug Abuse and AIDS Prevention
Underage Drinking Prevention

There are also many charities, educational institutions, and social service agencies that use advertising to inform people about public concerns or solicit contributions for research activities. If you watch television or listen to radio, you can't help but be exposed to these appeals on a regular basis.

Besides possible projects with the Advertising Council, almost every sizable agency, plus many advertisers and members of the media, have one or two civic, charitable, or educational projects that they back at their own expense and through asking the support of members of the media.

Many government agencies also employ advertising agencies to promote certain branches of the government. The largest share of these dollars is spent on advertising for the military: the Army, Navy, Air Force, and Marines. The Post Office employs adverting as a means to increase public use of the postal services. In fact, the U.S. government is one of the country's largest advertisers. This fact creates special circumstances for the advertising industry, since all dealings with the federal government are subject to a great many safeguards and regulations with commercial companies. In standard commercial transactions involving the advertiser and agency, oral agreements are all that is required to start things rolling, and large amounts of money are committed as a result of these understandings. On the other hand, when doing business with the federal government, an advertising agency cannot undertake any new projects or bind the government to any financial obligations without first completing a great deal of paperwork to provide legal authority for the plan. As a result of these restrictions, many advertising agencies employ specialists to deal with the administration and management of government contracts. This may be an area of special interest for some of those seeking a career in the advertising industry.

THE ADVERTISING JOB MARKET

The growth of the American economy in the twentieth century had a great effect on the growth of the advertising industry during the same period. The post-war boom of the 1950s and 1960s led to a great increase in the amount of money spent on advertising by American businesses. With more disposable income in the hands of Americans, businesses looked to advertising to spread the word about their products in order to cash in on the newfound spending habits of the public. In 1950 American businesses spent $5.7 billion on advertising, practically twice as much as was spent in 1930. By the late 1980s advertising expenditures had increased to over $120 billion, and by 1990 advertising spending reached a high of $128 billion. The recession of the early 1990s, however, had a great effect on an industry whose growth and opportunities seemed to be never ending. Many who predicted continued growth for the advertising industry were disappointed when the industry suffered its first decrease in spending in thirty years as total expenditures fell from $128 billion in 1990 to $126.4 billion in 1991. Though the industry rebounded in 1992 with spending increasing to $131 billion, the damage had been done. The recession coupled with the merger mania of the 1980s led to many lost jobs in the industry— 7,600 in 1991 alone. Even though the belt-tightening of recent years has limited the amount of opportunities in the advertising field, the industry appears to be turning around and greater growth looks to be in the future, as long as the economy continues its recovery.

Fewer entry-level positions exist in the advertising industry than before the recent recession, so the competition for these jobs can be fierce. Obviously the candidate who has prepared well for a career in advertising will fare the best in the quest for that coveted first job. Often the new agency employee starts out working as an assistant and learning the department operations from the inside out. For example, in the creative department, the *production assistant* learns print, TV, and radio production and art production while helping the rest of the department with general office work. This position has great growth potential. Also in the creative department, the *assistant copywriter* helps the copywriters with editorial and proofreading work as well as general clerical duties. Strong language and writing skills are needed for this position. In the marketing department, the *advertising assistant, sales* can gain experience with sales representatives and clients while handling heavy phone work and typing. The *media assistant* assists the marketing department in the area of media operations with buying, planning, and scheduling. This work can also include the preparation of graphs and charts and involvement in client presentations. The enterprising employee will do his or her best in these entry-level jobs, no matter how menial some of the tasks may be. Employees who are eager to learn the business and help their agency can look forward to being promoted and enjoying a long and rewarding career in the business of advertising.

CHAPTER 2

A LOOK AT THE MEDIA

The media are the form of communication used to convey the advertising message. The most widely used media include television, radio, newspapers, magazines, and direct mail. Other less commonly used media are outdoor posters and billboards, brochures, premiums, giveaways, and sampling.

Generally speaking, media are thought of as either national or local. Through the vehicle of national network television or national circulation magazines such as *Time* or *Newsweek,* the same advertiser can deliver the same message throughout the country in essentially the same form and at about the same time. Of course, even national ads can be localized to a degree. During a nationally televised ad, a local announcer can be heard on the screen giving a number to call in your area, or an advertiser can localize a message by placing a split-run ad in a national magazine or use the services of Media Networks, a division of the 3M Company, which sells, publishes, and inserts local metro ads in a wide variety of national publications to serve local markets. National advertising is utilized for products or services that are sold in the same form and under the same conditions in all parts of the country. Most consumer goods, including powdered soap, canned and frozen foods, automobiles, and other standardized products use national advertising. Some retailers with stores in all parts of the country also use national advertising media.

Local media are just what the name implies—media that serve a local audience. Local advertising is done on television and radio stations and through local newspapers and magazines. Local media appeal primarily to advertisers who offer goods and services only in a limited area, for example retail stores, banks, manufacturers with limited distribution, restaurants, and other service businesses. National firms may use local media to test market a new product or to advertise to serve specific area needs. For example, a national advertiser may run a local ad in order to list retail outlets where a particular product can be purchased.

TELEVISION

By far the most visible and most controversial advertising medium is television. Since its beginnings around 1950, television has grown into the largest national advertising medium with nearly $30 billion in revenue in 1992. Network television commercials advertise products or services that have nationwide distribution and that, for the most part, are financially within the reach of most people. By network TV we mean a number of television stations located in cities throughout the country that are affiliated with each other in order to carry the same program during the same time period. Similarly the same advertisements are generally shown with each program. Because of network television each participating station can telecast a wider variety of shows of better quality than it could produce on its own. Network television assures advertisers of program consistency as their message reaches all areas of the country.

Local TV is used essentially by retailers, automobile dealers, department stores, banks, and others. Commercials may appear on locally produced shows or as local spot commercials on nationally televised shows.

The advent and expansion of cable television has resulted in a variety of new opportunities for advertisers. Instead of choosing from three to five channels, the viewer now may choose from as many as one hundred or more channels. As a result, cable programming is able to serve the special interests of viewers so that a viewer may select programs devoted to specific interests. Because of this advertisers can now select an environment in which the advertised product fits well and will attract interested viewers. For example a cable TV series on gardening should attract viewers with interest in gardening. As a result it should be of interest to Scott's grass seed for sponsorship.

A TV commercial may take the form of a thirty-second spot that is almost always televised with one immediately following another (a practice known as piggybacking). Commercials of ten and twenty seconds are also common. So-called "station breaks," eight- to ten-second segments that appear between two programs, are another common form of commercials. Spots of one minute or longer, once very common, are now rare. On most television programs, commercials are spaced at ten- to twelve-minute intervals. Thus the average prime-time network program has a total of about nine and one-half minutes of commercial advertising.

Most of the shows or programs today are now produced by the major networks or are obtained from independent producers. A few advertisers still have a hand in developing their own shows, although this practice, common in early days of radio and television programs, now is extremely rare (another example of a major change in advertising practices).

Advertisers, with the advice of their own staff advertising and marketing people and of their advertising agencies, are very selective in the shows they sponsor. Advertisers may select from sports events, comedies, dramas, or special events and will seek an atmosphere or setting that will showcase the products they want to sell. In some cases, sponsors may even object to the contents of a particular program and withdraw their advertising rather than be associated with something they do not think will reflect well on their products.

On any given night one or more people in about half of the homes in America are watching television. Thus 100 million people or more could be watching an event at any one time. The success or failure of a television show, and therefore its ability to attract advertisers, depends on the percentage of the total number of people watching at any one time that are tuned into that show. These rating points show the "share" that the program receives. A widely watched program like the Super Bowl may have a rating share of over sixty percent.

Yet, even though most television programming and advertising is designed to appeal to the greatest possible number of people, some programs are aimed at more selective groups. Golf and tennis telecasts reach a high proportion of male viewers whose incomes, education, and job levels are substantially above average. As a result you'll find the sponsors of such programs to be advertisers such as IBM, American Airlines, or perhaps Hyatt Hotels. Pro football, baseball, and boxing telecasts attract a male audience that crosses all economic and educational levels, thus you'll find more beer and automotive advertising. Other programming may reach primarily female audiences and be sponsored by women's products manufacturers.

RADIO

Radio is the greatest mass medium of all. Although it is primarily a local medium today, radio broadcasts reach more people in more places and under more circumstances than any other media. The majority of homes in this country have two or more radio sets. In addition there are car radios, boat radios, portable radios, and even radios with headsets for walkers and joggers. Today automobile drivers and their passengers represent the largest segment of the radio audience.

Radio is used by national and local advertisers to promote goods and services that appeal to the masses and that are widely distributed and readily obtainable. For example, discount stores are heavy users of radio; Tiffany's is not. About 6.7 percent of all advertising dollars, or $8,654 million in 1992 are spent on radio. Nearly 75 percent of this figure is in local spot advertising.

Nowadays, there are only a few network radio programs on the air, so most advertisers who use radio to cover the whole country do so by buying spots on a station-by-station, city-by-city basis.

There are two somewhat specialized approaches to the use of radio for advertising. One is the early morning/late afternoon broadcasts that reach people driving to and from work. Since these are heard by large numbers of automobile owners, advertisers selling cars, tires, batteries, gasoline, and other products related to driving are heavy advertisers in these time segments.

The second consideration in the use of radio is related to the selection of stations according to their programming. A station featuring country music will have a loyal and definitive audience that appeals to advertisers who identify with that type of consumer. Some stations are aimed at special ethnic groups; others are beamed to identifiable age groups. The products advertised on such stations are the ones likely to appeal to the tastes of such listeners.

One other point about both TV and radio. All licensed stations are required by law to provide free time for messages "in the public interest," and each must keep a log that records how many of these spots were aired each day and at what time of the day or night they were broadcast. A great many of these messages are those sponsored by the Advertising Council.

NEWSPAPERS

Broadly speaking, newspapers are also mass media. The United States has about 1,800 daily newspapers and 8,500 weekly newspapers, plus innumerable neighborhood papers, religious and ethnic papers, and specialized papers such as *The Wall St. Journal.*

More than 60 million people each day read at least part of a daily newspaper. Newspapers accounted for approximately 24 percent of all advertising in 1991. Most newspapers are 65 percent advertising and currently account for over $32 billion worth of advertising a year. The desirability of advertising in a specific paper depends on rates, circulation, the market served, and the number of people who read it regularly. Advertisers and agencies gather the needed data from sources such as Standard Rate and Data Service and in discussions with newspaper advertising representatives.

Newspapers are the most timely of print media because they are published so frequently—daily or at least weekly. Thus a department store ad for air conditioners can appear the morning following the start of a heat wave.

Upwards of 85 percent of all advertising appearing in newspapers is placed by local businesses. Sections within each newspaper attract advertisers whose products relate to the editorial content. Thus, cake mixes are advertised in the cooking or food section, houses in the real estate section, fishing tackle in the sports pages, and so on. Newspapers carry two main types of advertising—classified and display. Display ads will range in size up to as large as a full page and most include illustrations. Classified ads, or want ads, often advertise jobs, real estate, or private goods for sale. Classified ads are usually only a few lines and seldom contain illustrations. Advertising agencies and advertisers generally prepare display ads; the classifieds are generally typeset by the newspaper.

MAGAZINES

Magazines are visually more attractive than newspapers and are usually published for a specific or target audience. The editorial content of magazines determines the audiences they attract. Each magazine is edited to appeal to the needs, interests, or tastes of a particular cross section of the public. *TV Guide,* which sells more copies than any other magazine, is edited for people with an interest in television programming and TV personalities. *Time* and *Newsweek* are current events magazines; *Tennis, Golf Digest, Fly Fisherman, Working Mother,* and *Historic Preservation* are even more specialized. You can probably think of a long list of others. Advertising people call these publications *consumer magazines.*

Magazines that provide information and technical data about specialized fields are called trade, business, or industrial magazines. Publications such as *Women's Wear Daily* or *Photographic Trade News* and even a magazine called *U. S. Glass* are classified as "trade" since they deal primarily with the news and changes in their respective field. Closely related are business publications such as *Advertising Age, Ad Week,* and *Business Marketing* that serve the advertising profession and publications such as *Folio, Publisher's Weekly,* and *Editor and Publisher,* each serving a segment of the publishing business. Industrial publications are generally more technical and would include titles such as *Electronic Products, Wire Technology,* and *Plastics Engineering.*

In addition to all of the above mentioned national magazines, there is a group of publications edited for local consumption. Such magazines on the consumer side include statewide publications such as *Texas Monthly, New Mexico, Connecticut,* and others, and dozens of city magazines such as *New Orleans, Los Angeles, Chicago,* and more. There are also successful magazines that cater to highly affluent local audiences such as *Palm Springs Life* for the resort community in California and *North Shore Magazine,* which serves the wealthy suburban communities of Chicago. The growth of local magazines has seen the birth of specialized publications such as *Michigan Florist, Crain's Chicago Business,* and others. These local magazines are growing fast and are receiving more and more attention from national advertisers who have a need to advertise locally and prefer the higher grade of paper and printing of a magazine as opposed to a local newspaper. Also these magazines generally serve a more upscale reader (higher income and education), which has appeal to certain advertisers. Many national magazines have responded to this trend by offering local metro editions that enable a national advertiser to place an ad in one or two local urban markets and not pay for the entire circulation. A great deal of information is gathered about the readership of successful magazines: the ages, incomes, educational levels, occupations, buying habits, car ownership, and other characteristics. This information influences the advertiser in the selection of one magazine over another and is the subject of constant debate among advertisers, agencies, and the magazines' sales representatives. Equally important is editorial quality, trends in circulation, the overall appearance of the magazine, and its standing among competition. Advertisers and agencies generally gather these data from the advertising salespeople.

Magazine advertising is generally favored over television for advertisers who wish to reach a specialized audience. For example a manufacturer of a $500 camera will find a well-defined market among the 650,000 people who every month buy *Popular Photography*. On television, which, of course, delivers a far larger audience, perhaps only 2 to 3 percent of the viewers might be interested in the camera. Cigarettes and liquor advertisers advertise heavily in magazines since they are banned on TV, and also because they often prefer the quality of printing and full-color reproduction of magazines over newspapers.

Over eight billion dollars were spent on magazine advertising in 1992—about 6.1 percent of all advertising dollars. Of this amount about 60 percent was spent in consumer magazines and the other 40 percent in trade and business publications.

OUTDOOR ADVERTISING

Outdoor advertising consists of two major forms of advertising. One is a twenty-four-sheet poster made of sections of heavy paper, generally known as a *billboard.* The other is a hand-painted display, called a *spectacular,* which often is lighted and animated. An outdoor ad for cigarettes on which an illustrated person seems to be blowing smoke rings is considered a spectacular. Normally twenty-four-sheet posters are changed every month, while the spectaculars remain in place much longer.

Outdoor advertising is aimed at anybody and everybody who passes by. Because it is difficult to determine who will pass a given corner, outdoor advertising is not as selective as other media. Of course, a billboard at the intersection in a plush suburb is more likely to be seen by affluent buyers than one at the main bus station in the city. For the most part, outdoor advertising is used by advertisers to carry short (six to eight words) reminder messages for low-cost, frequently purchased items with national appeal like soft drinks, beer, chewing gum, or tobacco products. It also is used widely by automobile makers at the time new models are introduced on the theory that this medium allows the new cars to be shown almost in life-size. Local advertisers use the outdoor medium for the same kinds of merchandise and also for localized services like banks and real estate projects. Smaller posters of varying sizes that are seen in airports and bus stations and on railroad platforms also are considered outdoor advertising and are referred to as *transit* advertising. These are used to advertise products relating to the activities of the people who view them—for instance, travel and hotel promotions, advertisements from Hertz and Avis, advertisements for luggage, and reminders from the phone company to call ahead or home by long distance.

An impressive amount of the space on posters and transit ads is devoted to causes supported by the Advertising Council. In all, the various forms of outdoor advertising account for about 0.5 percent of all advertising dollars, or approximately $1,031 million in 1992.

DIRECT MAIL

Direct mail advertising brings all sorts of information and advertising directly into your home or office, and it is one of the fastest growing areas of advertising. This medium comes in many sizes, shapes, and forms. At one end of the spectrum is what is commonly referred to as junk mail, which is simply addressed to "Resident." At the other are personalized letters, addressed to the recipient by name and bearing a real signature. Today, *telemarketing,* or sale of products and services over the telephone, represents a highly productive technique that is changing direct mail to direct marketing.

Direct mail may be in the form of letters, postcards, envelopes with various stuffers, booklets, catalogs, or bro-

chures. Because of computers and other highly sophisticated ways of compiling, maintaining, and sorting mailing
lists, direct mail is perhaps the most selective advertising
medium of all. There are available lists of people identified
by zip code, education, age, type of job, annual income
(i.e., "$25,000 or more"), ownership of season tickets to
the opera, and a multitude of other distinguishing factors.
Direct mail is used to reach from as few as two people to
as many as several million. Both local and national advertisers use this method to sell practically everything—from
a $10 solicitation to join the neighborhood Little League
to a $100,000 around-the-world cruise.

Direct mail is relatively more expensive than other major
media. The cost to reach a thousand people is used as a
standard measure. The return rate of people responding to
a direct mailing is often as low as a fraction of 1 percent.
But direct mail is particularly valuable to many advertisers
because its response is the most truly measurable of any
form of advertising. As a result of continuous testing of
offers and different copy approaches, the responsiveness
of different lists can be predicted with surprising accuracy.

Roughly 19 percent of the total spent in advertising
media goes for direct mail.

OTHER MEDIA

There are many other forms of advertising that also
should be mentioned. These include premiums, window
and point-of-sale displays, sampling, matchbook covers,

sound trucks, skywriting and airborne banners, and *shoppers*—the tabloid-sized newspapers that are hand delivered free to apartments and houses. There are no accurate estimates of the dollars spent in such miscellaneous forms of advertising, but these types of media account for millions of dollars every year.

CHAPTER 3

WHAT IT TAKES TO MAKE IT

What kind of person is likely to enjoy the advertising business and do well? This is the key question for any one having an interest in getting into the business or finding out more about it. This is true whether you are a student choosing a career or an adult planning a career change. It is most important that an interested person understand the answers and can assess her or his aptitude accordingly.

First, let's take a look at what advertising people are like. As with people in other fields, they come in a wide variety of sizes, shapes, talents, backgrounds, likes, dislikes, philosophies, and other human characteristics. If you have an idea that they are all turned out of the same cookie cutter, you are mistaken. They are not. Different advertising jobs require different skills, and the best advertising results from teams with the greatest range of talents, skills, and people. In fact, the head of one of the biggest and best advertising agencies once proudly described his company as being more of a menagerie than an organization.

PERSONAL CHARACTERISTICS

In spite of the fact that advertising people are as different as the members of any school or college class, those who do well have at least these common denominators—interest, imagination, initiative, energy, and a highly developed competitive instinct. Often they possess other similar traits.

Interest means a normal concern about the immediate job or assignment. It also means curiosity about people—what they do, why they do it, how they do it; curiosity about both our physical and social environment; curiosity about political trends and developments; curiosity about new (and old) products and services; curiosity about art, books, theater, fashions, food, drink, manufacturing, marketing, and business in general. And most important of all, anyone considering a career in advertising must have curiosity about changes in life-styles and patterns of human behavior and about attitudes that affect purchasing habits and the buyer-seller relationship. Good advertising people, like all good business people, must always be eager to improve their understanding and to re-educate themselves. In other words, they need to stay in touch with the ever-changing world around them.

Imagination means the ability to restructure former experiences as a way of developing new ideas and of approaching and overcoming difficulties. It means not only the ability to create new ideas but also the ability to recognize other people's ideas, to improve upon them, and to carry them through completion on schedule. Almost all the best advertising people keep their imaginations lively through interest, through curiosity, and through continuing self-education.

Initiative means being a self-starter. The dictionary defines initiative as "readiness and ability in originating action" or "taking action as a result of one's personal decision." To be successful in the advertising world, you must have this characteristic.

Energy means the stamina and willingness to put in long hours on frequent occasions. An agency performs a service. It and the people in it work for somebody else—the client. They must be ready to accept and carry out many difficult assignments on very short notice. Deadlines are an inescapable part of the business. So in those instances in which the client does not like the advertising that the agency has presented, it's "back to the old drawing board" with time running out and energy at a premium.

Competitive instinct means actively wanting one's products to succeed in the marketplace. It also means having a deep determination to develop outstanding advertising—advertising more exciting and effective than being done by the competition. Of course, all business is competitive; but perhaps none is more so than the advertising business, since the greatest opportunities for advertising agency growth and profit today come from getting new accounts, which are clients of other agencies. Almost every agency has a list of prospective clients that it is trying to wean away from competitors. Consequently, agencies must fight both to retain the business they have and to acquire new accounts.

Personal integrity. We know that all successful business and human relationships depend on the integrity of the people involved. In the advertising business, there are two circumstances that place a premium on integrity. The first is that because most dealings between agency and client, agency and media, or client and media are done on the basis of oral agreements, these must be honored scrupulously.

The second requirement for integrity is less obvious. In general, clients employ agencies to do more than simply produce advertisements. They are also supposed to develop marketing plans to help the client's business prosper, and they spend much time, thought, and research in doing so. Therefore, how well your ads perform can have a huge impact on the advertiser's success. If there is disagreement between client and agency, the agency representative or advertising manager must have the integrity to support his or her views with tact and determination. In a few words, you have to be able to develop thoughtful convictions and support them.

Dislike of routine. Most advertising people find that one of the greatest satisfactions of the business comes with many new opportunities and challenges. Most problems and assignments differ from all the others; few are more than superficially alike. Moreover, in the course of a career, an advertising person will learn about and become familiar with a variety of other businesses, each with its own unique problems and opportunities, its own particular appeal to consumers, its own channels of distribution, and its own trade practices and traditions. Variety is, in fact, the spice of advertising life. Therefore, those who are looking for a comfortable and predictable business climate need not apply.

Team spirit. Advertising recommendations almost always represent the combined contributions of a number of people. The business is, therefore, most satisfying to the person who enjoys being part of a team and who takes pride in group output.

Respect for other people's ideas. This asset is much like team spirit, particularly in working with one's agency colleagues. Clients also are entitled to their own views. Even when clients disagree with the agency, they deserve respect, understanding, and especially accommodation. Successful agency people are reminded to remember the golden rule. "He who has the gold makes the rules."

A wise old agency friend once put it in a nutshell. He asked one of his associates who was in violent disagreement with an advertiser's viewpoint, "How come we have all the brains, and the client has all the money?"

Ability to communicate. This is obviously essential; without it there is no hope of planning or executing successful advertising programs. Ideas are usually very hard to put into words in a satisfactory and understandable way, and failure of written or oral communication makes the advertising business almost impossible. On the other side of the coin is the need to be able to understand what others are saying and to figure out what they mean. This ability can be perfected through practice, but it is a good thing to have an aptitude for it from the beginning.

Sense of humor. The advertising business is more of an art than a science. Consequently, there are many honest disagreements about what is effective and appropriate advertising and what is not. The head of a large advertising agency once said that fifty percent of all advertising is effective and fifty percent is not. He went on to add, "The only problem is that no one knows which fifty is which." When disagreements take place between the client and the agency, the client is almost always the sure winner. If you happen to be a casualty of such a situation, you need to be able to laugh off your disappointment or at least grin and bear it—for you can be sure this will happen throughout your career. Although you should always take your job seriously, life will be easier for you if you have enough of a sense of humor not to take yourself too seriously.

SALARIES

There is a popular belief that everybody in the advertising business makes a great deal of money. That is not necessarily the case. Many beginners earn salaries that are lower than similar positions in other businesses. Since there are so many young people trying to get into advertising and communications, it is very much an employer's market. A junior copywriter may earn as little as $20,000, while a junior account executive may earn around $25,000. However, once people become firmly established, the salaries become disproportionately higher. At these higher levels, the personal relationships between account executives and the clients often influence the advertising agency's profits, and as a result, successful agency people can command well over $100,000 a year. Outside of advertising agencies, salaries for those working in corporate advertising departments are usually slightly better for beginners and slightly lower at upper levels, except for situations where the corporate advertising director is among the top officers in a corporation. In such instances, he or she will command a very high salary including corporate perks. This is more likely to happen in firms dealing with consumer products such as liquor, cigarettes, perfume, and others where the company's success is much more dependent upon good advertising and promotion.

Beginning wages are, however, much better now than they were a generation ago. In those days, the biggest and best agencies started their trainees at scandalously low pay on the theory that it was a privilege to receive training from such outstanding institutions. They almost took the view that it was condescending of them to pay anything at all. That philosophy has gone, and starting salaries are now reasonable.

The American Association of Advertising Agencies and other organizations conduct periodic surveys of how much member agencies pay their employees by function at various levels of responsibility. These surveys show that salary scales generally are comparable from agency to agency. The only exceptions are adjustments for the cost of living in different parts of the country and a tendency for smaller agencies to pay somewhat less than larger ones.

There are good reasons why the average agency person does not make as much money as some people would think. In the first place, between two-thirds and three-quarters of the cost of running an agency is its payroll. Therefore, the lower the payroll expense, the greater the profits for the owners. Secondly, agency income can be cut sharply by client decisions to reduce advertising appropriations, in which case a top-heavy payroll becomes financially unmanageable. Consequently, well-managed agencies try to get along with as few employees as possible in order to avoid having to lay off many people in hard times. Additionally, it is thought to be wise to keep salaries at a sensible level and to supplement them with some kind of bonus arrangement when profits in a given year increase.

1993 Advertising Salaries

Position	Salary
ADVERTISING AGENCIES	
Chief executive officer	$139,934
Creative director	$ 95,792
Art director	$ 52,193
Chief copywriter	$ 52,231
Media director	$ 55,794
Senior account executive	$ 69,312
Account executive	$ 42,349
MARKETERS	
VP marketing	$126,666
VP product manager	$ 98,269
VP brand manager	$ 91,875
VP advertising	$ 99,761

Source: *Advertising Age,* December 6, 1993.

FRINGE BENEFITS

In many jobs, there are, of course, other benefits besides base pay. It is not possible to suggest that there is any conformity in the way that different agencies handle fringe benefits because an examination of the policies and practices of a large number of agencies proves only that no two are alike. On the other hand, there are certain fringe benefits that are common to most of the larger agencies, even though the specifics may differ.

- More and more agencies now offer profit sharing to provide nest eggs for employees who stay for a number of years. Although the terms of these agreements are not all the same, the basic principle is each year to deposit an amount of money equal to a given percentage of each employee's annual salary in a trust fund in the name of the employee. When the employee retires or leaves the agency for some other reason, whatever is in the trust fund in his or her name is paid over, in accordance with the terms of the agreement. Relatively few agencies have pension plans because profit-sharing plans are properly thought to be more rewarding to both short- and long-term employees.
- Group life insurance is a common benefit.
- Many agencies pay the full cost of travel and accident insurance for their employees.
- Practically all agencies provide hospitalization insurance. Though this coverage may be completely paid for by the agency or by the employee, often the cost is

shared by both. The same is true of major medical (catastrophe) insurance.

- Many provide long-term disability insurance either wholly paid for by the agency or shared by agency and employee.
- As you go up the ladder, almost all agencies have some sort of an executive bonus or profit-sharing arrangement. The amount distributed depends on the profit performance of the agency in a given year and management's assessment of each person's contribution to that performance.
- Since entertaining clients and prospective clients is such an important part of the business, fringe benefits will often include country club and city or lunch club memberships, company cars, and a rather liberal attitude toward entertainment and travel expenditures. Therefore, you will find that top-level agency people are often found in the best hotels and restaurants and often travel first class on their air trips.
- Finally, ownership of stock in the agency is another prerogative of advancing responsibility and represents still another way of building up savings toward the day of retirement.

If you find yourself working in the advertising department of a large corporation, you will generally find the fringe benefits similar to what is standard in your particular industry.

CHAPTER 4

THE ADVERTISING AGENCY: INSIDE AND OUT

There are three parties involved in developing and executing advertising. They are the *advertiser,* the *advertising agency,* and the *media* that will carry the advertising. This chapter focuses on advertising agencies—their functions and structure, the opportunities they offer, and the kinds of people they employ. For the record, however, there will also be brief sketches of advertising jobs and responsibilities in corporate advertising departments, in media operations, and in other businesses related to advertising.

There are over 6,000 advertising agencies in the United States today, ranging in size from one- or two-person shops to large agencies, operating with one or two thousand employees. Larger agencies generally offer a complete range of services from market research and public relations through direct response services and print campaigns, television production, and worldwide marketing. Some small advertising shops may simply provide layout and design for simple print ads, and even then they may send out some of their work to freelancers. However, whether they are large or small, most functions performed in every advertising agency are similar. It's just that in the small firms, one person may act as account executive, creative director, copywriter, and artist.

In this chapter we will explore some of the jobs performed at advertising agencies. We will also investigate some of the principal positions that exist in many agencies and describe the functions that each performs. We will discuss equally important opportunities in corporate advertising, public relations, and the media. Of course, in this brief overview, we can only touch on a few of the many jobs that make up advertising.

AGENCY FUNCTIONS

What does an advertising agency do to earn the money it is paid? Its primary responsibility lies in planning, creating, preparing, and placing advertising on behalf of its clients in whatever medium is believed to be best suited to the purposes of the advertiser. In order to carry out these assignments successfully and professionally, the agency must be organized in a way to perform certain basic functions. They are:

Agency management. As in any business, someone has to be in charge—someone who can provide the required leadership, make the final management decisions, set the policies, and see that policies are carried out. In the larger agencies, it is usual for a president to be the chief executive officer, reporting to a board of directors. In smaller agencies, the principal owner usually sets the policies and sees to it that they are carried out, just as in any other small business.

Account management. The job of working day-to-day with the client, of preparing and presenting the agency's recommendations, and of reporting the client's views and wishes back to the agency is carried out by account executives, account supervisors, and account managers in agencies with clients big enough to support two or three levels of account management. In agencies with smaller accounts, such responsibilities are carried out by one or two people who will generally carry one of these titles.

Creative services. A combination of writers, artists, producers, and other creative talent work together to create broadcast commercials and print advertisements and other needs such as packaging, displays, and other forms of advertising. In some of the larger agencies, activities such as fashion coordination, casting, and talent direction also come under this heading.

Traffic control and production. The function of these jobs is to make sure that all the necessary printing and reproduction materials, transcriptions for radio spots, and film and tapes for television commercials are prepared on schedule to be submitted to the client for approval and furnished to the media in time to meet their deadlines.

Media services. Specialists analyze, evaluate, and select the medium or media to be used for an advertising campaign (magazines, newspapers, radio, TV, outdoor, and so forth) and the individual publications, stations, or networks that are best suited to the objectives of the advertising plan. Media directors, space buyers, time buyers and their associates spend considerable time meeting with the representatives of the media and attending media presentations to learn more about what is available.

Publicity and public relations. In those agencies that have such units, the assignment calls for the need to organize and execute programs that will build the client's image and procure publicity for client products or services.

Sales promotion. Some large agencies have a separate department for developing point-of-purchase displays, product packaging, and many other items and devices designed either to draw attention to a product in its retail setting or to enhance the performance of the client's sales force.

Direct response. More and more agencies have people who specialize in the development of direct mail material and programs. Some agencies specialize in direct response, and many large agencies have direct response subsidiaries with names like Ogilvy & Mather Direct.

TV program production. Just a handful of agencies have staff specialists whose assignment is to develop and produce television shows or specials. This activity has expanded and will continue to expand as a result of the opportunities in cable television. More and more advertisers are interested in shows that are built around their products and services.

AGENCY COMPENSATION

As has been noted, agencies act on behalf of the advertisers they serve. Today most agencies are paid a fee for their work. This fee may be paid on an assignment-by-assignment basis—the cost of the work of completing each ad or series of ads is billed separately.

In other cases, agencies work on a contract that will generally include a specific budget. The client and the agency agree to carry out specific tasks over a given period at a specified cost. The cost of each individual ad and the production charges are charged to the client, but the cost is not to exceed the sum agreed upon in the contract. Agencies sometimes are asked to bid on a project, such as a new catalog, and will then contract to complete the project for that sum.

Agencies also are compensated in part by charging a commission, or add-on charge, on materials or services bought from outside suppliers—artists, photographers, printers, film producers, and other such independent operators. The usual add-on for these outside purchases is 17.65 percent of the suppliers' charges, which translates to 15 percent of the total amount billed to the client. This amount covers the cost of arranging and managing the details. Furthermore, fees are charged for such things as publicity and speech writing, sales promotion work, staging and conducting sales meetings, and any other nonadvertising service that the agency may perform.

In most cases, the advertising agency also receives a 15 percent commission on media placement. The exceptions include retail ads in newspapers and other "noncommissionable" media. If a full page in a magazine costs $1,000, the publication bills the agency for $850. The agency retains the $150 commission and bills the client the $1,000, the amount the client would have to pay if dealing with the media directly. The amount retained by the agency provides income to the agency and may be the only form of income the agency receives from the client. In other cases the client will pay the agency an additional fee or if the client is a fairly large user of commissionable space or broadcast time, may insist that the agency perform certain services in return for keeping the large commissions. As the advertising business has become more competitive, it is now quite common for large advertisers to negotiate media commissions. Many large clients allow their agencies to retain only 12 percent and expect rebates or other services to make up the difference between the 15 percent commission the agencies receive from the media.

ACCOUNT EXECUTIVES

The functions of an account executive (AE) and her or his account supervisor (AS) are both demanding and diverse. To be good at such jobs, a person must combine sound business judgment and a high level of proficiency in advertising. The AE is responsible for the following.

Planning. The AE must plan the advertising for the client—the job that the advertising is to accomplish, the idea or ideas that are to be communicated, the people (audience) to be reached, the media to be used to reach them, the frequency of such use, the amount of money required to get the job done, and the standards for measuring the campaign's effectiveness if such measurement is to be undertaken.

To do this job properly, the AE must become an expert in the client's field of marketing, The AE must know the sales and profit goals set by the client, the industry of the client's business, the channels of distribution that are used, what the competition is spending and doing, and how well it is succeeding and why.

Because account executives must deal more with economics and statistical and financial information and because they must analyze more complex data, an increasing number of advertising account executives and other client contact personnel in agencies hold MBA degrees. Twenty years ago, most AEs were super salespeople who acquired the business skills on the job. But as advertising becomes more firmly rooted in statistics and business, more and more AEs will be required to have advanced business degrees.

Coordination. Since the agency recommendation is the product of contributions from many different specialists, it falls on the AE to make sure that all the parts are brought together on time to form a creative whole. In doing this, the AE must oversee the work of creative people, media specialists, producers, researchers, and often, outside suppliers. This means that the AE must have a thorough working knowledge of the responsibilities of each of these people. The account executive essentially serves as a catalyst between the agency staff and the client.

The AE must be a good judge of copy and must be sure that the advertising to be shown to the client is precisely on the right track and does not stray from the objective of the campaign. The AE must have an appreciation of art and layout design, in order to judge material to be presented to the client. In short, a good account executive must be an imaginative and sound critic whom colleagues respect.

The AE must understand the strengths and weaknesses of the different forms of media and be able to translate this knowledge to the assignment at hand. This means having good reasons why magazines, say, are best for a client's needs.

The AE must be up-to-date on production requirements for both broadcast and print media and the costs and time elements involved. He or she must be familiar with a variety of research sources and techniques and understand their applications, using good judgment regarding what research can discover and when to use it. If the agency is engaged in point-of-sale and packaging, the AE must be well informed about sources and what works best.

Finally, and most important, the AE must know and understand the people he or she works with—the members of the team—and must have a feeling for the problems connected with their jobs and an ability to motivate and stimulate them to do their very best work.

Presentation. The account representative is generally responsible for presenting the agency's recommendations to the client. In this capacity, the job has two parts. First, when an advertising campaign is underway, the AE will have frequent, often informal, meetings with the client to discuss details and to present new commercials or written copy. The matters discussed may include the extension of media commitments, analysis of the budget, and minor changes in wording and art treatment. Second, when the time comes to present a new plan or campaign, one that departs from the course that has been followed, the process becomes much more formal. The agency usually makes a presentation to explain to the client the reasoning behind its new proposals and to show samples of headlines, layouts, and concepts. In such meetings, there are apt to be a number of client people present, who are not normally involved in the day-to-day advertising transactions.

In this situation, it is up to the account person to decide on the physical form that the presentation will take. Is it to be a formal presentation with slides and flip charts, or is it to be a low key discussion around a conference table? Is the proposed advertising to be in its final finished form, or is it to be indicated by rough layouts and storyboards? How many agency people will participate actively in the presentation, who will they be, what role will each play? This phase of the account person's work is a little like being a theatrical producer and director combined.

Regulatory matters. As set forth earlier, there is a growing body of governmental regulations controlling the content of advertising. The modern account executive must be familiar with this expanding body of rules. He or she also should be familiar with the various codes and practices of publishers, stations, and networks in order to be in a position to negotiate with them on matters affecting the client's interests.

Profit management. In addition to all the other duties and responsibilities, the account executive is responsible for the profitability of each account. Does it make money for the agency, or does it not? The agency management will always be ready with reminders that if the agency does not operate at a profit, it will not operate at all and that every account is supposed to contribute to that profit. Accordingly, the responsible account person must monitor the quantity of manpower and time that each account absorbs and maintain a minimum consistent with the high quality of service to which the client is entitled.

In all of the preceding discussion, the term *account executive* has been used to cover the broad spectrum of assignments that come under the heading of account management. As agencies grow in size, however, it is necessary for them to have more than one level of account responsibility. Thus, the bigger ones not only have account executives, they also have account supervisors to whom several account executives report; in many cases they have management supervisors to whom both account executives and account supervisors report. All of these people, at whatever level, have the same responsibilities as those outlined. Aside from the need for satisfactory internal agency management, the different levels are required to match the organizational structure of the agency's clients. In this way, the management supervisor does business with the vice-president of marketing, the account supervisor with the director of sales and advertising, and the account executive with the advertising manager.

CREATIVE SERVICES

The reputation and profitability of the advertising agency is made or lost in the area of creative services. Although all the functions of an agency are important and contribute to the success of the plan or campaign, the end product—the advertising itself—is what the client is most interested in, since that is what the public sees or hears and either responds to or ignores.

The people in the creative services department are writers, designers and art directors, and commercial producers—specialists in supervising and managing the production of print ads and radio and television commercials.

In many agencies today, these people work together as members of a team, and any one of them can be the originator of a bright new campaign, a brilliant idea, or some approach that stimulates the reader or viewer to go out and try the product or use the service that is being advertised. Each member of such a group should be a first-rate advertising professional as well as a topflight technician in one or more specialties. And with a team operation, each member tends to stimulate and motivate each other to better and better work.

Even though it is often hard to tell who is finally responsible for the finished advertising in a team effort, there are still specific skills that each specialist must have.

Writers. Writing must always be clear and persuasive and must be aimed exactly at the people being addressed. It may be formal, informal, or technical; but it must clearly convey the idea called for in the underlying advertising plan. When promoting products, the best writers create advertisements that contain one simple idea expressed clearly, memorably, forcefully, and persuasively. When the job is to communicate more complex ideas, writers must present them clearly, logically, and convincingly. Very few writers are equally good at both tasks, and most feel more at home with one than with the other.

Writers must also have a well-developed understanding of design and illustration and what they contribute to the power of the written word. They should recognize the fact that the illustration is often the most important element in an advertisement, and that their writing must fit the visual aspects of the presentation of an idea. They also must have a feeling for the techniques of commercial production and be able to imagine how they can contribute to the excellence of the finished commercial.

Writers must understand the uses and lessons of copy research in order to take advantage of those techniques that are known to be most successful in capturing the viewers' or readers' interest and attention.

Like account executives, writers must have a current and thorough knowledge of all the legalities affecting the claims that can or cannot be made for the product or service being advertised. Writers are not solely responsible for following all these rules and regulations, of course, but competent writers will assume such responsibility in order to avoid possible trouble.

Writers need the enthusiasm and the curiosity to get out into the marketplace and see what is going on. They need to find out what their clients' competition is doing, what consumers are doing and thinking, and what "the trade" (storekeepers, clerks, salespeople, distributors, wholesalers, and agents) are up to and what concerns them. In short, the best writers always have a very clear concept of the environment in which their advertising appears.

Writers also need to get to know their clients and to become well acquainted with their ideas and their products. Often writers will be called on to present personally their recommended advertising, supported by the thinking and analysis that went into its development. Writers who are good at this job will find such proficiency of great assistance in their career development.

In big agencies, creative departments require management and supervisory activities. Groups or teams of creative people usually are headed by a group supervisor who directs the activities of the people in the creative group, assigning projects to them, monitoring what they do, and editing and polishing their output. These supervisors report to a creative director, one of the most important people in an agency and almost always one of its principals.

Designers. This word is a catch-all for those who design print advertising and direct the video part of television commercials. They create the illustrative material that makes the advertising come alive, capturing the attention of the reader or viewer.

Designers have special skills and talents, just as writers do. Some are best at designing for the printed page, while others excel at creating television commercials. Looking first at the print side of the business, it is obvious that people working in this field must be adept at arranging elements of type and illustration so that they are harmonious, clear, uncluttered, easy to read, and effective in getting the advertising message across quickly and accurately. Designers must understand different typefaces and sizes and how they contribute to the readability of the layout. If these details sound a little exaggerated, look through any magazine or newspaper and see for yourself how some advertisements are much more attractive and readable than others.

Designers also need a sense of what kind of illustration will make the greatest contribution to the effectiveness of the finished advertisement. Should photography be used? Should it be a cartoon? Should it be a painting? Should it be a drawing? Whatever it is, should it be bold or muted? Again, these may seem like minor considerations, but the answers have a very pronounced effect on the final product.

Once the decision as to the right art form has been reached, the next step is to decide which artist or photographer is best qualified to produce the desired effect. Larger agencies sometimes have art buyers to help with this chore, but in most cases designers must perform the task themselves.

A background of training in an art school or a school of design is a must for those engaged in this kind of work. It is imperative that designers be able to draw or sketch well enough to demonstrate to the client a clear idea of how the finished advertisement will look, even though someone else will do the finished artwork.

It is easier to describe the skills needed by persons working with the printed page than those needed by top-flight television commercial producers. While print designers have a limited range of design alternatives from which to choose, producers of commercials have available all the processes and devices of film and sound recording—animation, superimposition, close-ups, long shots, fade-ins and fade-outs, stop motion, slow motion, studio effects, on-location scenery and backgrounds, and a host of other optical tricks. To be fully professional, producers must be familiar with them all and must know which one is most likely to reinforce the persuasiveness of the message and still fall within the approved budget for the job.

Production of commercials is an art form calling for great sensitivity and imagination. The best commercial producers may have a preconceived idea of the desired effect when they start to shoot a commercial. Although some experimentation is possible, it must be limited if costs are to be controlled. The job can be compared to that of both the director and producer of a Hollywood movie.

Commercial producers must also decide on the jingle, the sound effects, or the background music used in the commercials. Working in conjunction with the casting director, the commercial producer must also select any performers that are required.

Casting directors screen applicants for parts in commercials and select those who seem best suited to the established requirements. Casting directors must keep files on available talent and must know all the talent agencies and the kinds of actors and actresses they represent. They must be proficient enough in the field of television to be able to evaluate the appearances, mannerisms, and voices of performers as they relate to the mood and purpose of each commercial to be produced. Additionally, casting directors must spend many hours auditioning and screening prospective talent.

TRAFFIC CONTROL AND PRINT PRODUCTION

In some advertising agencies, traffic control and print production functions are combined; in others they are kept separate. Either way, they work together so closely, it is often difficult to determine exactly where one leaves off and the other begins.

Traffic control. This department can be likened to the air traffic control tower at an airport. It is the place where timetables and deadlines that govern everything that happens are monitored. Traffic control is responsible for seeing that all the pieces of an advertisement are fitted together and forwarded to the designated medium in the proper form and on time. The material can range from the type and illustrative elements needed for engravings or photo reproductions for print advertisements to electrical transcriptions for radio commercials.

Traffic control personnel in an advertising agency often work under considerable pressure because, as deadlines approach, time is almost always short. All the other steps in writing, designing, presenting, and securing client approval of the advertisements usually consume whatever extra time may have been available. Above all, good traffic planners must be orderly and well organized. They need to be able to manage a great amount of detail accurately. They must know all about the different processes that are involved in the creation of an advertisement, with special emphasis on the amount of time needed to complete each step along the way. They must also be able to keep track of and move along a quantity of projects all at one time.

They must be able to deal effectively with outside suppliers and with the members of the creative team with whom they work. They must know which creative people respond to coaxing and which ones need a firmer hand in order to get them to attend to the details most of them hate but which are essential to the completion of the traffic control department's job.

Traffic control can be a demanding job, but for those who enjoy it and do it well, it provides the satisfaction of knowing that it is the indispensable lubrication for the agency's gears.

Print production. The production people are responsible for buying the various elements that go into the makeup of every kind of printed material produced by the agency—advertisements, booklets, pamphlets, brochures, outdoor posters, flyers, presentations, sales manuals, direct mail material, and any other form of printed matter. The production people deal with a large number of outside suppliers who offer a substantial range of services and materials. These include typographers, engravers, electrotypers, photo reproducers, photostaters, printers, and sometimes, freelance artists. As a result, production people need to have source files of all the available facilities for each of these services and must know the strengths and weaknesses of each supplier.

One of the key responsibilities of print production employees is budget control. Therefore, they need to know not only whom to contact to get a job done, but how much it is likely to cost. In many cases, it is necessary to get competitive bids, particularly on large or complicated assignments and on all government contracts. This requirement usually means extra delays and extra record keeping.

Like traffic controllers, good production people need to be well organized and capable of close and accurate attention to the details of a number of projects that may be processed simultaneously. The production employees must also be "certain sure" of the amount of time each supplier needs to get the job done under normal circumstances, as well as the absolute minimum each needs under the most urgent pressure that can be brought to bear.

Both traffic control and print production can be career jobs for those who find them sufficiently satisfying and rewarding. For the most part, however, they are learning jobs that function as stepping stones to better paying jobs in an agency, usually in account management.

As an important aside, in past years, almost everybody in an agency started in one of these jobs. This is no longer true, but it is essential that account people, writers, and designers really understand what print production and traffic activities involve and how essential they are to the smooth operation of the agency.

Art buying. As noted earlier, this job is closely related to both design and print production. Buying the artwork that will be used to illustrate the finished advertisement demands knowledge, taste, and negotiating ability, as well as the facility to get along well with the creative people for whose output the art is being purchased.

There are many parallels here to the job of the casting director. The art buyer must have extensive information about the talents of a large number of commercial artists from photography to oil painting to cartooning. Buyers must also know who is best qualified to do dramatic photographs of heavy machinery and who is best at fashion photography.

Art buyers must keep a roster not only of specialties but of subspecialties as well.

Art buyers are also constrained by deadlines, and therefore must know who among the available artists or photographers can be counted on to deliver on time and who is likely to exceed the time available. Buyers also are governed by budget considerations and therefore must be able to negotiate prices that are acceptable to clients. In carrying out this responsibility, good business judgment is a must. Art buyers must be sufficiently well organized to keep the records necessary to make the job run smoothly and professionally.

Art buying is a fascinating and gratifying occupation for anyone who has a true appreciation of the whole spectrum of commercial art, who enjoys dealing with interesting and talented people, and who gets satisfaction from discovering and helping to make a success of aspiring young artists

MEDIA SERVICES

In order for advertising to be effective, it must be seen or heard and acted upon by the right audience—the people most interested in the product or service. It makes no difference how good the advertising is; if it does not reach the target people, it is relatively worthless. This is where the media department and media services come in. The media department of an advertising agency has the responsibility of evaluating, selecting, and recommending the publications, stations, and programs that will expose the advertising to its greatest advantage. And since clients take a greater interest in media matters than in any other, except for the advertising itself, media buying is a vital link in the client/agency relationship.

Media services perform three major functions—research, selection, and buying. As we have already outlined the attributes of the major media categories, let us now continue with a broad description of how a media operation works and the kinds of job opportunities available.

Media evaluation. The process begins with media research. Every agency of any size has a basic research library, and large firms subscribe to a great many different research services. These services supply huge amounts of data on reading, viewing, and listening habits, as well as profiles of the readers and viewers of various publications and programs.

The primary source book for the basic information about newspapers, magazines, and radio and TV stations is *Standard Rate and Data Service,* commonly referred to as "SRDS." It lists all the publications and stations, giving circulation and viewer information, costs of different units of space or time, any discounts that may be earned by the use of more than one spot or advertisement, and coverage of each station or publication. For many years, this was the only source of reliable information about the media, but there were some things that it did not report, like the ages, incomes, life-styles, and buying habits of media audiences. Services such as the Nielsen service, MRI, and Simmons now provide this more sophisticated type of information. Others attempt to measure something known as psychographics. This includes people's likes and dislikes, attitudes and beliefs, prejudices, and patterns of use of one product or another.

In simple terms, what this means is that a car manufacturer like Buick or Volvo can have some assurance that their new car advertising is aimed at the right type of buyer and not directed at used-car buyers. Until recently, it was very hard to have any degree of assurance about such distinctions, but computerized data banks have greatly increased our ability to store and sort many pieces of information.

In today's agency, the computer contributes greatly to media research and selection. Let us consider an advertiser with a large budget and an advertising plan specifying the use of magazines and network TV to reach women between the ages of twenty-four and thirty-five. The aim is to reach the greatest number of such women the greatest number of times within that budget. The media selector puts together a list of magazines and programs that are good possibilities for the assignments and turns the list over to the research staff. The researchers feed the information into the computer, and the computer reports back the combination of those media that will get the desired result with the greatest efficiency.

There are also extensive files of other more commonplace data in the agency's media research library. This information includes material obtained from the radio and television stations describing the characteristics of their audiences.

Media researchers are more than just keepers of these records. They must be able to evaluate all this material and decide how much of it is reliable. This skill requires that they understand the techniques used to collect their data and whether such techniques are valid. They make the final decisions about which research services the agency will buy or subscribe to and the extent to which these services will be used. Their jobs require imagination and analytical minds that find statistical investigation fascinating and challenging.

Media selection entails using the available information to put together, in the most precise way possible, the combination of media that will be seen or heard by those people most apt to respond to what the advertiser has to offer. The task starts with an understanding of the basic advertising plan—the audiences to be reached, the requirement for repetitive force, the length of the message to be used, and the money available to do the job. This understanding is fundamental for effective choice.

Media selection. The first step in media selection is to single out one or more categories of media that generally fit the requirements of the ad campaign. From that point on, the buyer, with the assistance of the researchers, refines the pattern until it is tailored exactly to the proper specifications. Although it may not seem so, selection is more than a job of juggling numbers until they come out right. With the use of imagination and a good understanding of available media, the process of media selection can become quite creative.

In addition to the data available in the research files, selectors are continually receiving sales presentations by representatives of the various media. In order to stay up-to-date, they must spend a considerable amount of time in discussions with these media salespeople and assess the validity of what they have to say.

Good buyers must be analytical, comfortable with figures, imaginative, interested in the broadcasting and publishing businesses, well-informed about them, and alert to the importance of the intangible (or unmeasurable) aspects of each medium and submedium. As in every other advertising job, buyers must also be eager to find innovative ways to do work that is unusually constructive and sophisticated in nature.

Media buying. Media buying is an extension of selection. It is relatively easy to buy space in a magazine or a newspaper because most publications have unlimited space for sale. It is, however, not so easy in the case of radio and television time, particularly television spots. In these media, buyers are given the specifications against which to find the best spots for the advertiser's purposes. They then find out from the stations or their representatives what spots are available; these are known as "avails." When this information is in hand, buyers negotiate for the purchase of those "avails" that will best meet specifications and budgets. Since the rates asked by most broadcasting stations are quite flexible, purchasing is truly a matter of negotiating, and professional and knowledgeable buyers can stretch their clients' budgets substantially by skillful negotiation. Frequently buying is done on the basis of oral agreements, which then are confirmed in writing. For this reason it is absolutely essential that both buyers and sellers live up to their agreements scrupulously.

Good buyers must be good handlers of detail, good data analysts, and good workers under pressure. When buyers get busy, they get very, very busy, even by agency standards.

Buying is often a stepping-stone to selection, supervision, or more senior management jobs, although there are some people who choose to make a career of it and who do very well financially.

Within advertising agencies, media personnel spend a tremendous amount of time with advertising salespeople who represent the media. Such representatives are either employed full-time by the media (such as the major networks like NBC and CBS who have their own staffs), or, in the area of broadcast, they are employed by independent representative organizations such as John Blair in radio and television. A firm like The Hennessey Group specializes in the representation of magazines and has trained advertising sales personnel. These salespeople receive training in the demographics and buying characteristics of the readers of the magazines they represent. Thus they can assist the advertising agency's media personnel in assembling and evaluating the data required for their media recommendations.

MARKETING

The marketing function has been the subject of far too much analysis and discussion in recent years, and it is really more of an advertiser's job than that of an agency. Nonetheless, nearly all bigger agencies and many mid-sized ones have marketing departments, usually as counterparts to the same kinds of departments in their clients' organizations.

In simple and realistic terms, marketing is the process of planning and organizing the making of a product that people want, at a price they can afford to pay, and in the form that they like. Then they must see that it is sold through the kind of outlets where the consumer would expect to find it. If you have ever sold lemonade on a corner, you understand the marketing concept. You pick a hot spell, set up your stand at a busy place, add sugar to suit the customers' tastes, and charge what you think people are willing to pay.

Marketing departments generally do some or all of the following:

- They try to find openings for new products that fit the producer's manufacturing and distribution facilities.
- They try to find ways to improve existing products to make them even more salable, often characterizing them as "new or improved."
- They look for new uses for established products, like using baking soda to deodorize refrigerators.
- They look for new buyers for a product by seeking new markets, perhaps in foreign countries.
- They study the successes and failures of competitors' products in the marketplace.
- They may have a merchandising unit that, by modern definition, is concerned with promotional opportunities for a product at the retail point of sale. Such a unit develops special packaging; posters; display devices; incentives for dealers, retailers, and salespeople; contests; giveaways; cents-off deals; coupons; sampling; and tie-ins with related products and other promotions that they believe will increase sales.

Market research, though still more often undertaken by the advertiser, frequently is carried out by the agency or by a specialized research firm.

Marketing research, the basis for modern marketing decisions, involves determining what areas of opportunity are open to a manufacturer and the kinds of packaging, pricing, distribution, and promotion that will make the manufacturer's product successful. The following is a list of the major information sources utilized by market researchers:

- Government statistics, an incredible source available to everyone.
- Trade, business, and industrial magazines that serve specific fields.
- Business statistics assembled by various trade associations and business groups.
- Client information, which is the private and often closely guarded property of the company to which it belongs.
- Syndicated services that provide information on the movement of an advertiser's goods and those of competitors on the retail market. Without these services, it is very hard to tell what is happening to products after they leave the factory. This is particularly true in the case of packaged goods such as cosmetics, prepared foods, drugstore items (aspirin, tobacco products), and many more.
- Visits to the "trade," which involve going out into the marketplace and finding out what dealers, retailers, and salespeople are doing to help or to hinder the sale of an advertiser's product. This kind of investigation is of particular value when a number of competitive products—like washing machines—are sold in the same stores. Salespeople can have a vital effect on sales of such items in the way in which they present different brands.
- Specially commissioned private research that gives readings on the attitudes and behavior of various consumer groups. This type of study is valuable when the manufacturer is not too clear about consumer attitudes but knows they are important to successful marketing.

If people in marketing are to be successful, they must keep asking themselves two questions: "Why?" and "How can we use what we know to make the client's business more profitable?" Topflight marketing personnel must be imaginative, practical, and businesslike. They must be knowledgeable about the marketplace and must work diligently to keep up with what is going on in it. They must be enthusiastic followers of trends and developments in consumer attitudes, opinions, habits, and life-styles and must have a good idea about what makes people tick. They should be clear and persuasive communicators, both orally and in writing. Finally, they must have the kind of curiosity that makes marketing exciting and enjoyable.

OTHER AGENCY JOBS

In addition to the highly specialized functions of an advertising agency or of the advertising department of an advertiser, as in any other business, there are a number of other things that must be done. They are briefly discussed below:

Financial management. Every agency places contracts and insertion orders with various media each month. Because these orders obligate the agency to generally pay out several times more money than the agency has on hand, it is customary for the client to pay the agency enough to cover these media bills before they appear. If anything breaks down in this arrangement, the agency can find itself in serious financial trouble. Therefore, the job of managing the cash flow of an agency is one of major importance.

Most agencies have at least one person who is responsible for monitoring their cash positions and for ensuring prompt collection of bills and prompt payment of supplier invoices. The larger agencies have both a treasurer and a controller who assume these responsibilities, They, in turn, are backed up by the necessary clerical, secretarial, and supervisory personnel, whose qualifications are the same as those for similar jobs in any other business.

In-house legal counsel. In view of the fact that laws and regulations affecting the advertising business are in a constant state of development and refinement, most large agencies have one or more lawyers on their staffs as advisors to the account management and creative department personnel. Agencies that specialize in highly regulated commodities, such as pharmaceuticals or securities, are more likely to retain in-house attorneys. They also are the link with whatever outside legal counsel the agency may employ. This is a very highly specialized form of law, which can be fascinating and challenging because of the formative nature of the rules that govern the advertising business.

Office management. This function is just what it sounds like. As in any business, management is essential to the proper functioning of the agency. It involves all the housekeeping chores of the business and, frequently, also includes direction of the personnel operation.

Basic support. Like every other business, agencies need secretaries, typists, clerks, receptionists, librarians, and information specialists. If the agency has a computer network, it needs all the programmers, analysts, and technicians that any other computer installation requires.

Although the tasks involved in advertising support jobs are similar to support positions in other types of business, the atmosphere in the field of advertising can be more lively and challenging.

CHAPTER 5

CREATING ADS: HOW IT'S DONE

Having just discussed the many different functions performed in an advertising agency, we will focus now on how all of these different people with all their various skills work together to create ads. Although there are many different types of advertising, including billboards, packaging, and point-of-sale displays that are created in advertising agencies, space limits us to two of the broadest and most common types of ads created in agencies—print ads and television commercials. To some extent the types of work will overlap, particularly at the early planning stages. Once the actual production of the different ad forms begins, however, specialized skills come into play.

RESEARCH

The first step in developing both print and broadcast advertising is research. We have already discussed some of the jobs performed by those people who work in marketing research. There can be several principal goals of initial market research on a product or service. The advertiser or the advertising agency needs to determine what the target market is and how the product should be presented to most effectively appeal to that market. Basic exploratory research uses statistics of the company, government data, information from trade associations, discussions with representatives of the media, and possibly information from independent research organizations to develop a clear picture of the people who buy the product; how the product is perceived by the consumer; what they like and don't like about this or similar products; and how much money is spent on the product.

Market researchers may also use direct methods of research, including telephone interviews, experimental use of the product, or questionnaires prepared by on-site interviews.

ADVERTISING PLAN

Using the information gathered by the market research department, the account executive, the creative director, the project copywriter, and other agency members work to develop an overall advertising plan for the advertising being created. First the account executive and supporting staff working with the advertiser, develop the overall goals of the advertising campaign. Of course the ultimate goal of most campaigns is to sell more products, but often the advertising goals are generally spelled out in more detail.

For example, Belltower Advertising may set some of the following goals for the new Speedo soap that XYZ Company is introducing.

In one year we want to:

1. Communicate the existence of Speedo to the approximately fifteen million consumers of liquid washing detergent.
2. Inform at least 50 percent of those consumers that Speedo is a high-quality, competitively priced product that will allow them to wash their clothes more thoroughly at little or no extra cost.
3. Convince at least 40 percent of that 50 percent (of the group aware of Speedo) to actually purchase a trial size of the product at a local retailer.

Once advertising goals are established, the account group, consisting of an account executive, an art director, and their respective support staffs, begin to use its creative talents to develop a concept for the advertisements. The ad concept must be geared to reach the target market. In this case women between twenty and forty-nine must be completely convinced that the product has the benefits outlined in the research—fast action and high quality—so that they will consider buying it.

Once the concept has been developed, each separate group within the creative department—copywriters, scriptwriters, and designers—begins working on how best to convey this message in effective ads. Often the initial concept of the ad partially determines what medium will be used. Of course, the media department will also do research that will help determine the chosen medium.

Some ad campaigns run very similar copy on both TV and in print, but for purposes of this discussion we will treat each as a separate entity.

PRINT ADS

Copy

Although it is nearly impossible to separate the importance of the copy in a print advertisement from that of the illustration, good copy still remains the backbone of most successful ads. The first task of the copywriter, when presented with an account, is to understand completely the objectives and strategy of the advertising. This knowledge is essential if the copy is to market the product successfully. Next the copywriter concentrates on coming up with several headlines, or leading statements in the ad, that convey the essential selling points of the product. In some agencies, copywriters prefer to write the headline and then the copy; in other agencies, copy is written first and headlines are taken from the content. These headlines will be used later as the largest copy in a print ad. A good headline should both convey the message of the product simply and succinctly and grab the reader's attention. Most headlines tend to consist of only a few words that can be quickly read and remembered. Sometimes headlines are witty, based no doubt on the theory that if it is clever one is more likely to remember it.

Once the headline has been developed, the copywriter goes on to writing the body or main copy of the advertisement. These interior paragraphs of copy must tie the headline to the remainder of the ad and at the same time must clearly state the main benefits and selling points of the product. As well as describing the virtues of the product, the copy must also inspire the reader-consumer to action, which usually means "buy the product." This portion of the copy, known as the *close,* is essential to every ad regardless of whether that ad is trying to sell a product or simply instill an idea.

Design

During the same period that the copywriter is developing the written material, the designer is developing the visual for the ad. However, the order to this procedure varies; sometimes copy is based on an existing visual. Often the design depends to some extent on the intention of the headline, so the artist may not begin work until at least the headline of the ad has been written. Once some idea has developed on how the ad should look based on the advertising strategy and any preliminary copy, the designer develops one or more rough layouts showing where each of the elements that make up the ad will be positioned in the final advertisement. The layout includes a rough drawing indicating what the photographs or illustrations will look like, where the copy and headline will be placed, and the location of any design elements, such as the company logo or symbol.

Mechanical

Once the layout and the copy have been reviewed and approved by the art director and the account executive, the copy and a more carefully drawn example of the ad, called a *comprehensive* or *comp,* are shown to the client for review. This process can involve a complex presentation or may be handled more informally, but generally before any further work is done on the production of the ad, the client's approval must be obtained. Once the copy and design have been finalized by the advertiser, the agency prepares a mechanical of the ad. A mechanical consists of all of the elements of the ad placed in exactly the position and size as they will appear in print. To create the mechanical, the agency first has the copy set in the type style and size indicated by the designer. This job is usually handled by an outside firm, or typehouse. However, with computerized typesetting, many agencies are setting some of their copy in-house. The copy is then proofread for mistakes by an in-house proofreader and all mistakes are corrected.

The photo or illustration to be used is created and a copy is placed on the layout. The actual processing of the photo into a printed page is handled by the printer. If the illustration or other parts of the ad are to be done in color, the color or colors are indicated on sheets of tissue that overlay the ad.

Printing

In some cases where an advertisement will be inserted into a magazine or newspaper, the mechanical is sent directly to the publication for inclusion. In other instances, the magazine requires that a negative used for printing be submitted. This job is handled by the advertising agency, which arranges for a separation to turn the mechanical into film form. In the description below we describe the process of preparing material for printing on an offset press. This is the most popular form of printing in the United States today. If other types of presses are used, plates are prepared in a slightly different way.

Using a special camera, the separator shoots film negatives of the mechanical. A separate negative is shot for different colors used in the process. Black and white pages, like those in this book, require only one black plate. If a full-color ad is being created, the separator creates four plates—black and the primary colors of red, blue, and yellow. Through the mixing of these primary colors, all colors can be created. In many cases the negative created by the separator is sent to the magazines and newspapers that will run the ad.

In instances where the ad is being printed by the advertising agency (as is often the case when an advertising insert is placed in a publication or used as mailing piece), the next step in the printing process is photo platemaking. The platemaker creates plates showing the appearance of each of the negatives and how they will combine to create the ad. Proofs of these negatives are studied and corrected by the ad agency before printing. The material is then ready to be plated and printed. The paper used in printing is selected by the designer to meet the size, weight, appearance, and cost requirements of the ad. The printer uses the specified paper to print the ad. The printed materials are then dried, folded by a machine to the desired shape, and cut to the size indicated by the designer. Then the finished ad is shipped to its destination. In some cases printers will run some sample copies of the piece through the press and send them to the agency for review before printing the entire run. This check gives the account executive and the art director a final opportunity to correct any errors.

BROADCAST ADS

Up to a point, the development of a printed advertisement and a broadcast commercial for television or radio is very similar. In both cases, the agency and the advertiser use market research to determine the target audience and the selling points of the product. In both cases, the data are used to develop an advertising strategy. Similarly, a concept is then created, which the agent and advertiser hope will convince the consuming public to buy the product. It is at this point, however, that the work done for a printed advertisement and a television commercial take separate paths. Instead of headlines and body copy, the copywriter must develop a script for the ad. And rather than a layout, a storyboard is developed for the commercial.

Scripts

A television script is divided into two parallel portions. On the right side of the page, the writer indicates the sounds that will appear in the commercial, including all spoken dialogue, music, and sound effects. On the left side of the script, the writer indicates what images are seen on the screen during the period when each sound is heard. For example:

Visual	Audio
Middle-aged housewife standing beside washer on which rests a bottle of Speedo	*HW:* Doing the laundry used to take all day Saturday. But not anymore.

Many of the same rules for writing advertising print copy effectively also apply to scriptwriting for commercials. The opening statement should be brief and should attract the audience's attention. Situations should be believable and simple enough so that the story of the commercial does not interfere with the ad's principal function—selling the product. Moreover, the scriptwriter should remember that in a television commercial the pictorial portion of the ad carries more than half the weight in the audience's mind. The written material should support rather than dominate the commercial.

Design

Just as with print ads, the design of the commercial is generally created after at least a preliminary script has been approved. At this stage the art director and the writer prepare a storyboard. A storyboard is just what it sounds like, a series of drawings mounted on a board that shows the major action that takes place in the commercial. The number of frames in the storyboard varies from eight to about twenty depending on the complexity of the commercial. The spoken portion of the commercial, plus any instructions regarding what the scene should look like are printed at the bottom of each frame. The storyboard serves as a guide to the actual shooting of the commercial.

Production

Once the script and visuals have been approved by the client, production begins on the project. Here again we refer to commercials using live actors and actresses. Commercials using animation, special optical effects, and other production specialties are handled by various specialized professionals.

The first step in production is for the director of the commercial (either an employee of the agency or an outside expert hired to produce the spot) and the art director to begin casting the commercial. Actors and actresses who generally fit the descriptions of the characters in the commercial are auditioned and hired. Next, sets and outside locations, if needed, are selected and assembled. If outside locations are used, necessary permits are obtained. All needed props and wardrobe, including a large supply of the product to be advertised, are assembled. The director and the agency determine what sorts of technical personnel are needed for the commercial. Camera operators, lighting and sound technicians, make-up artists, hair stylists, and stagehands to move the scenery are among the people needed to produce even the simplest commercial.

On the day of shooting, light and camera crews may spend several hours setting up and lighting the set. During this time, the director may help performers develop the proper reading of lines and the action needed for the commercial. Long delays may occur between each scene for relighting and rearranging the set. All in all, shooting a one-minute spot can take up to a day or more.

Postproduction

In the postproduction phase, the many little pieces of film and sound created by the director are assembled to form the finished commercial. The film is edited into the correct order and the sound that has been recorded during the shooting is synchronized with the visual. Any recorded voices, music, or sound effects are added at this point. After a final review by the agency and the advertiser, the film editors complete the final, or answer print, of the commercial. The film is then duplicated and sent to television stations that will televise the commercial.

THE WORK OF MANY

As you can see, creating an advertisement, no matter how simple it may seem when you look at it, requires the efforts of many people. These people must work as a team to produce commercials rapidly, creatively, and within the costs defined by the client's budget. Even this brief survey does not begin to cover all of the many people inside and outside the agency who contribute to the creation of the advertising you see.

CHAPTER 6

EDUCATION: PREPARING FOR YOUR CAREER

There is probably far less agreement about the proper educational background for a career in advertising than about many other professions. The days when a talented high school student could get a beginner's job in an agency and learn completely on-the-job are nearly a thing of the past. Although on-the-job training is still a valuable part of any advertising professional's education, college training in advertising, journalism, or marketing has become a necessity in order to enter the field of advertising today.

Since the importance of communication in advertising cannot be overlooked, even the person who is not planning on becoming a copywriter should benefit from courses and activities that lead to both oral and written communication proficiency in the English language. Otherwise, a good foundation in the basic high school subjects is a wise first step in preparing both for college and for a job in advertising.

COLLEGE

It is at the college level that theories about what courses to take to prepare for a career in advertising begin to differ sharply. There are those who strongly recommend that students take all available advertising courses, majoring in it, if possible. Others, including the author, believe it is better to elect a broader curriculum. Of course, selecting the appropriate courses to study for an advertising career is also difficult. To some extent, course selection depends on which facet of advertising you are thinking of pursuing. If you want to become an account executive, for example, you will need courses in marketing, speech communication, business and finance, as well as in advertising theory. On the other hand, if you want to become a designer, courses in drawing, illustration, and keyline are essential. And for all students, general courses are essential.

Few observers would dispute that advertising people need to know a lot about a wide range of topics. Therefore, it makes sense to get at least a grounding in a variety of subjects as a starter, rather than to narrow the academic focus to one specialty. Some understanding of all the following is desirable: history, English literature, psychology, economics, sociology, one or more languages, art appreciation, and music. In a college requiring students to major in a single discipline, an attempt to crowd in all these would impose a heavy load; nevertheless, all are valuable.

So, you are entitled to ask which of these should be your major; and here we again come to an area of disagreement. Some vote for psychology; some for business, business administration, or marketing; some for English. There are valid arguments in favor of each position, but English and speech are the author's two choices for a couple of reasons. The first and most obvious is that they are the best possible courses to train a writer, a speaker, or a communicator of any kind. Keep in mind that the basic commodity that an advertising person has to offer is ideas—and ideas are very difficult to explain and support, unless they can be set forth in clear and precise language.

The second reason may not be as obvious, but it may be even more pertinent. A series of courses in English literature is an unsurpassed opportunity to follow the development of the habits, attitudes, and aspirations of the people who speak a common language. It is a way to learn history as it was seen at the time it was happening. A major in English provides a way to gain insights into psychology, both mass and individual. It is a great trip through the social and economic changes that have brought us to where we are today. Clearly, this is not a vote to exclude courses in other subjects that contribute to a broader understanding of our culture and environment, but it is a reasonable proposition that appeals to a substantial number of advertising practitioners. Extracurricular activities such as work on school papers, yearbooks, and other college activities that involve media and promotion will also prove beneficial.

If you are interested in a career in advertising, perhaps the soundest recommendation would be for you to talk over your strengths and capabilities thoughtfully with your school counselor or placement officer. If you are returning to school to study advertising, school or independent career counselors can still provide useful direction. Such discussions will help you decide which course to pursue. If you decide to attend a college that offers a degree in advertising, a list of such institutions can be found at the end of this book.

AFTER COLLEGE

Next comes the question of postgraduate work. Is it a good idea to get an advanced degree in an area such as journalism or business administration? Once more we find that opinions differ sharply. Some advertising people still believe that additional experience gained by going to work immediately after college outweighs the benefits of postgraduate education for most advertising professionals.

Others in advertising believe that the increasing complexity of and competition in advertising makes an advanced degree more essential than ever before. If anything, postgraduate education seems to be more desirable for people interested in becoming account executives, marketing directors, or media specialists than for those interested in pursuing careers in the more "creative" portions of the business. This need grows out of the increasing importance of financial analysis and statistical research used in these areas. MBAs, once a rarity in advertising, are becoming increasingly common, especially in larger urban agencies. Advanced degrees are less in demand for people pursuing careers as artists and copywriters, although here, too, further education can always be of benefit.

In any event, the decision to go on for a graduate degree after college is a very personal one. The decision will always be affected by financial circumstances, marital status, eagerness to get started, interest in some subspecialty of the business, and other personal considerations.

To illustrate the wide variety of educational and occupational backgrounds of some successful advertising people, let's look at just one agency. Three of its top people did not go to college at all (this would be extremely rare today); others had these backgrounds: Protestant minister; police sergeant; golf professional; career soldier; automobile sales representative with a degree in economics; lawyer; sales engineer; magazine editor now serving as an account supervisor; people with bachelor's or master's degrees in advertising, business administration, journalism, communication, and liberal arts; psychology professor; graduates of art schools and schools of design, some serving as creative directors, some as account supervisors, and some in their original specialties.

This broad spectrum of backgrounds and training leads to only one conclusion—it is nearly impossible to prescribe any one, *right* way to prepare for the advertising business. But those who do well in advertising all have the common personal characteristics of curiosity, imagination, initiative, energy, and competitive drive. In advertising, these abilities prove ultimately to be more important than formal education.

PREPARATION BEYOND
THE CLASSROOM

Extracurricular activities are also an important part of your educational preparation. The greater their number and the closer they relate to some phase of advertising, the better. The ones that come to mind first include working on school and college papers, magazines, and radio stations, either on the editorial side or the business side. By all means, try to get involved in some aspect of one of these activities; they will help you become familiar with the realities and challenges of the communications media.

During summer vacations, try to find a job within the media or with a printing plant or a film studio, even though your assignment may be lowly and the pay very modest. Selling ads for local high school or college papers will provide valuable experience in selling and interacting within the business community. Another part-time or summer job that can be helpful in the long run is that of an interviewer for a research organization, which enables you to do consumer research. If you are in a community in which there is a chance to get this kind of work, you will soon find out how hard it is to get people to answer questions sensibly. Additionally, you will have a chance to study the structure and technique of the questionnaires as they affect people's ability and willingness to respond to them. It is useful experience.

Many advisers suggest part-time employment in any form of retail selling—from check-out counter to filling station—that will give you a chance to see how people behave at the point of sale. It is a way to see the real world of marketing and selling in action, and it will supplement theory and book learning in a practical way. In addition, such experience will help you when you compile a résumé for potential employers. (More about that later.)

Finally, many of us find it almost paralyzing to stand up in front of a group of people and address them. But the ability to speak on your feet is a must in the advertising business, and it is a good idea to prepare yourself for this task as soon as possible. It is wise to take courses in public speaking, to join a debating society, or to take part in amateur theater. Such activities help put you at ease and help develop "presence" in front of an audience.

In addition to these organized activities, you can prepare for an advertising career in your own way, at your own convenience, and at your own pace. All you have to do is to ask yourself questions about the advertising that you see every day. To whom is this advertisement supposed to appeal? What are they supposed to do about it? Is there one central message they should get from it? (If you think there is not, do not be alarmed; the fault is far more likely to lie with the advertisement than with you.) Is the advertisement trying to sell an idea, or is it endorsing the specific competitive merits of one product as opposed to others in the field? Is it trying to ride a trend or fad? Is it realistic or too farfetched? Is it contrived, or is it natural?

Ask yourself, in essence, why the advertisers created the advertisement the way they did. It is easy to play this game, and after you get in the habit, you may be surprised how much you can learn about advertising. If you find that you enjoy it, you may also find yourself trying to improve on the output of the professionals. This could be your first big step into an advertising career. Why not give it a try?

ON-THE-JOB TRAINING

Training in Entry-Level Positions

As was mentioned earlier, it used to be customary for a beginner in an agency to start in either print production or traffic. In earlier days, the mailroom or the secretarial pool were also considered good places to begin, although it is hard to see why. Some agencies still put their newcomers into print production or traffic, but the length of time they stay there is usually quite brief.

Today, it is more common to find beginners starting out in media, in research, in production, or in a training program that systematically moves them from place to place. In this manner, it is certain they will have an opportunity to become familiar with the various agency activities before being given their first real job assignments. Training programs differ from agency to agency in the sequence of departments observed, he length of time devoted to each one, and the amount of actual participation (as opposed to observation) in each one. Bearing in mind that these differences do exist, a more or less typical course of instruction might include the following topics and activities grouped within departments.

Traffic and Print Production Department
1. Agency procedures.
2. Assignments.

3. Dealing with other departments.
4. Printing processes, including tours of printing and engraving plants and typesetting shops.
5. Planning and buying print material other than advertisement—booklets, brochures, posters, displays, etc.
6. Legal requirements.
7. Security regulations and procedures.
8. Correspondence, mailing, and shipping.

Marketing and Research Department

1. Gathering and analyzing market information.
2. Developing a marketing or advertising strategy.
3. Designing market research procedures and questionnaires.
4. Using and reporting the results of market research.
5. Using copy research in its various forms for both print and broadcast.
6. Identifying and evaluating competitive media research.
7. Measuring the reach (number of people who see or hear the advertising) and frequency (how often they see it or hear it) of various media choices and selecting from various media alternatives.

Media Services Department

1. Fitting the media plan and strategy to the marketing and advertising goals.
2. Evaluating and contracting for network programs and spots.
3. Evaluating and buying market-by-market programs and spots.
4. Evaluating and selecting the magazines and newspapers that best fit each advertising plan.

Creative Services Department

1. Understanding how advertising is designed to fit the specifications of the plan and what thinking and discussion go into developing the plan.
2. Learning how the illustrative material is chosen and the sources from which it may be obtained.
3. Understanding how a TV commercial takes its form, from rough idea, to storyboard, to the finished product, including visits to film studios, animation studios, and on-location filming.
4. Learning how a radio commercial is made and about different techniques available, including visits to recording studios.
5. Casting and talent selection.
6. Codes and rules of the involved guilds.
7. Legal and regulatory restrictions and guidelines.
8. Budget control.

Account Management Department

1. Duties and assignments.
2. Formulating a marketing strategy.
3. Fitting the advertising plan to the marketing strategy.
4. Reporting the results of client meetings, including assignments for action to be taken.
5. Dealing with agency personnel in other departments.
6. Managing the client's advertising budget.
7. Directing agency activities for a profit.
8. Legal and regulatory consideration.

If the agency is engaged in promotional or merchandising activities, there may also be some instruction in these areas. It would probably include these topics:

1. Special requirements of sales promotion copy.
2. Sales promotion art and design.
3. Organizing sales meetings, including presentation techniques.
4. Using premiums, giveaways, contests, and selecting suppliers for these items.
5. Finding and taking advantage of publicity opportunities.
6. Legal and regulatory requirements (very important here because each state has different rules with respect to contests and premium offers).
7. Managing the budget.

It is clear that there are different theories about how best to train beginners and help them learn all the things they need to know. The important thing to remember, however, is that whatever system is used, it will be only as effective and valuable as each trainee's interest and application permit it to be. If the desire to learn the advertising business is strong, it really does not matter that much how the training program is designed. In addition, it should be remembered that such programs are only the beginning. For the true advertising professional, the learning process never stops.

Large mass-marketers of consumer goods (particularly in the food field) such as Proctor & Gamble, General Mills,

Kellogg, and others offer excellent training grounds in advertising. There is a definite advantage to such positions in that one learns of the actual movement of goods from a client's point of view. In a large corporation, the experience gained can be very useful in later work in an advertising agency. By working within commercial and industrial businesses, one can learn about the effects of an advertising campaign on the movement and profitability of goods over a long period of time. This experience does not necessarily have to lead to agency work; there are many good opportunities within business for lifetime positions in advertising.

CHAPTER 7

JOB OPPORTUNITIES

Having prepared for a career in advertising with a college program designed to give you both a broad general knowledge and expertise in some facet of advertising, you are now more than ready to get your first job and begin practicing the skills you have acquired. Since advertising agencies rarely interview on college campuses, it is up to you to go out and find a job with the type of organization that interests you.

Of course, this is much easier to say than to do, especially for the beginner who probably has little or no work experience and few if any samples of work. Remember, however, that more than in most other professions, you can show what you can do by creating samples of your work on your own to show to potential employers. These samples, if they are really well done, have a good chance of attracting employers, especially when combined with your enthusiasm and willingness to learn.

GETTING STARTED

Before applying for your first job, decide what you want to do or be in advertising—the kind of job that would work out best for you and *for your employer.* The emphasis here is important, because you must never forget that the job hunter must always focus on what can be offered that is valuable to the potential employer. In simple terms, the question to be addressed is, "What can I do for you?" *not* "What can you do for me?"

In deciding what kind of a job you are best suited for, you should try to analyze your strengths and weaknesses. What do you do well? What kind of useful and applicable experience have you had? What kinds of things do you like to do and why? What do you dislike doing and why? Are you impatient with details? Are you inclined to be analytical and careful? Are you at ease with people, or do you prefer to stay in the background?

This kind of self-analysis is useful and not nearly as difficult as it sounds. But it does take deliberate thought and a totally honest appraisal of yourself. When you have completed the self-analysis, you will be in a position to zero in on the kind of assignment for which you are best qualified. You may also find that you have some weaknesses that you should work to overcome. It is not a bad idea to check your findings with someone whom you respect and trust to verify your decisions.

Next, you should find out where the kind of job you want is most likely to be found. Then make your plans to cover that territory. If you want to work for a big agency, concentrate on major advertising centers like New York, Chicago, Detroit, Dallas, Denver, Minneapolis, or Los Angeles. If you think a smaller agency may be the best place for you, look around in some of the less populous cities. The *Standard Directory of Advertising Agencies* will give you locations and sizes of different firms. Reading trade publications such as *Advertising Age, Ad Week,* and *Business Marketing* and studying the help-wanted ads in order to see which agencies landed new accounts may give you an idea of which firms are looking to hire.

RÉSUMÉS

After you have pinpointed the type of job you are interested in, you must prepare a résumé outlining your qualifications. Most people approach this task with considerable apprehension, no matter how far along they are in their careers. The challenge in writing a résumé is to say enough to arouse interest and convey assurance that you are truly a qualified applicant, without overstating your accomplishments and abilities in a way that is likely to turn off your potential employer. Remember, advertising is communication and selling. Here is your chance to show how well you can sell yourself. It will help if you follow these basic rules:

1. Be concise.
2. List relevant employment and activities in reverse order. (The most recent one first.) Be sure to include

part-time jobs you had, especially those in sales or media that might be pertinent to advertising. Often these job experiences are more important than your academic achievements.

3. Try not to overstate or understate achievements. If you are modest, do not forget that the person looking at your résumé can only make a judgment on the basis of what is written. If you are inclined to be a little exuberant, remember that exaggerated claims are sure to reduce your credibility. Be as objective as possible.

4. Include academic achievements and extracurricular accomplishments. Be sure to include any evidence of leadership qualities (class officer, team captain, etc.) as these qualities are always in demand.

5. Record information about pertinent hobbies or leisure time activities, like painting, photography, short story writing, or music composition. These things are closely related to the work in advertising.

6. Do not forget to include your address and telephone number(s).

7. Give references that include the names, titles, and addresses of three or four people whose judgments and opinions about you are likely to carry some weight.

8. Prepare your résumé on standard size $8\frac{1}{2}'' \times 11''$ white bond paper. It is easiest for people to handle.

The following sample résumé should be helpful to you.

RÉSUMÉ

Myra A. Terry
612 Linwood Avenue
Springfield, Illinois 46149
Phone: (302) 555-2491

Employment Sought
Account Executive Trainee

Education Background
College: University of Illinois, B.A. in English, 1994.
>   Minor: Advertising
>   Honors and Activities: honors graduate, college radio station (4 yrs; 1 yr. as business manager), debate team, drama club president

High School: Tecumsah Senior High School, Peoria, IL
>   Graduated June 1990
>   Honors and Activities: assistant editor and official photographer for school newspaper

Employment Background (Summer employment only)

1993	1992
Lederer Research Company	Glenn's Car Wash
443 Wickham Way	324 Broadway
Peoria, Illinois 61611	Peoria, Illinois 61642
Mr. Robert F. Chin	Mr. Richard Cress

References

Ms. Juanita Valdez	Mr. Hutchings T. Looney
Vice President	Holmgren, Hascall & Wartell
Mutual National Bank	1647 West Main Street
Springfield, Illinois 46146	Peoria, Illinois 61604

Of course, if you have had one or more full-time jobs, you should list them, saying what you did, what your responsibilities were, and citing any bona fide accomplishments. Additionally, if you were part of a team that did something noteworthy, mention it. However, be sure to give the credit to the team effort and do not claim that you did it all by yourself. Personnel people are very skeptical of such claims and are likely to consider them, and the person who makes them, as transparently exaggerated. It is not worth the risk.

To accompany your résumé, it is a good idea to write a letter setting forth the kind of job you hope to get and adding some detail as to why you believe you are qualified for it. Do not, however, say anything about your salary. Such discussions come after you and your future employer have agreed that there is a mutually acceptable opening for you.

If you have letters of recommendation (or of commendation), either attach copies of them to your résumé or make them part of your portfolio. The more evidence you have of your employability, the better.

Never hesitate to ask personal and family friends or former employers to provide you with introductions to anyone who might have a job for you. They probably will be happy to assist you, and the contacts they provide will help you to broaden your network of associations in the business.

PORTFOLIOS

In addition to a résumé, you should also prepare a portfolio of your best advertising work before you set up any interviews. Here again you may face the problem of not having very many published samples of your work to include. Do, however, include articles you have written for the student paper and projects you prepared for class. But do not include any sample unless you feel it represents your best work. If you don't have enough samples, create some. The thing most likely to attract any employer to you is your creativity. How good are you at coming up with original, sparkling ideas? In creating ads for your portfolio, you need to demonstrate these qualities.

Study familiar products and try to come up with a novel way to sell one of them. Do some research on the product to determine its present, and possibly unknown uses. Study what benefits the product has for you and other consumers. Just as you would for a real advertising campaign, base your ad on what you learn.

What you include in your ad also depends on what type of job you are seeking. If you want to be an artist, the design of the ad should be of primary importance. This does not mean that you need to do an absolutely finished ad, but do complete your samples in a finished enough form to show that you can draw. And don't fail to include at least a headline for your ad.

On the other hand, if you see yourself mainly as a writer, the design for the ad does not have to be as well drawn, although you should clearly indicate the illustration part of your ad. Concentrate on writing a striking headline (or more than one) as well as at least part of the body copy— the explanatory copy for the ad. In both cases, if you have any knowledge or experience in doing television production, scripts and storyboards showing the major frames in your ad can also be included in your portfolio. An excellent book to use as a reference in preparing your portfolio is *How To Put Your Book Together and Get a Job in Advertising* by Maxine Paetro, who worked as creative manager for Foote, Cone & Belding, or *How to Succeed in Advertising When All You Have is Talent,* by Laurence Minsky and Emily Calvo.

INTERVIEWS

Once you have prepared your résumé and portfolio, you are ready to set up your first interview. Try to get an appointment with the agency's creative director copy chief or the head of any other department that interests you. Personnel people are not as likely to be interested or impressed with your work as department heads. When the time for the interview arrives, always be punctual. Remember, good manners and proper dress are recognized quickly, and first impressions are important, especially in a profession that emphasizes "image."

Interviews can be nerve-racking experiences because often you are expected to do most of the talking. The line between "running off at the mouth" and not saying enough can be a very thin one, particularly if you encounter an interviewer who silently stares at you. Consequently, you should consider what you want to communicate and carefully organize what you are going to say. Your emphasis should be on why you want a job *with this company* (not why you want a job; the interviewer knows that) and why you believe you are qualified for the position.

Go prepared with intelligent questions about the kind of work available and the contribution you can make. Do research about the prospective employer before the interview. Listen to the answers and try to create a dialogue. Ask questions that encourage the interviewer to talk with you. The interviewer will like you better if you can get her or him to do some of the talking. Whatever you do, *do not* focus your questions on such things as vacation policies, employee benefits, or anything else that suggests that you are more interested in what the company can do for you than in what you can do for the company. The employer will provide this information usually near the end of the interview. If it is not offered, the appropriate time to discuss it is *after* the employer has had an opportunity to bring it up. Before leaving, determine when you might learn the outcome of your interview. Ask if you may phone back in two or three days. Make an effort to keep the door open for future contact. If employment seems unlikely, ask the interviewer if he or she knows of an opportunity at another company. You may pick up a good lead that could help you to land your first job.

Unfortunately, few job applicants are hired at the first place they visit, and trying to get on someone's payroll often is time-consuming and discouraging. For those reasons, neither let your initial hopes run too high nor your early disappointments run too deep. Getting the right job, like most other worthwhile achievements, requires a systematic approach, hard work, determination, and persistence in your efforts.

ADVANCEMENT

Once you have been hired, you will soon start thinking about promotion and advancement. Here again, it is impossible to set down any definite guidelines. Advertising is not like the federal civil service in which so many years at one job level entitle an employee to move up to the next higher spot. How fast you progress in advertising depends almost entirely on your performance, ability to acquire the necessary skills, maturity, and grasp of the business. It is impossible to make any absolute statements about how quickly and to what level a new employee will advance in the advertising business; however, here are some general observations that apply to most beginners.

Do not expect to begin your advancement immediately. If you are hired right out of college as a trainee, it will probably be a year or two before you find yourself working full-time at some specialty—account work, media, research, creative work, or whatever. From that point on, your progress can be rapid, if you are capable and if there are not a number of equally competent people ahead of you.

A résumé for Robin L. Quint might look something like this after a few years on the job.

RÉSUMÉ

Robin L. Quint
430 Belden Lane
Chicago, IL 60606
Phone: (312) 555-0903

Employment Sought: Assistant Account Executive

Employment Background

1994   Assistant Copywriter
Wolfe and Facinelli Advertising
1000 Michigan Avenue
Chicago, IL 60600
Mr. Christopher Edman
Wrote body copy and some headlines for Pepsi
and Speedo detergent accounts.

1991–1993 Media Researcher
Wolfe and Facinelli Advertising
1000 Michigan Avenue
Chicago, IL 60600
Ms. Fran Horner
Worked for media buyer and evaluated
media and markets for clients in the travel
field.

Education Background

College: University of Illinois
B.A. in English, 1991
Important Courses: psychology, history,
French and Spanish

Honors and Activities: honors graduate,
college radio station (4 yrs; 1 yr. as business
manager), debate team, sorority president

High School: Tecumsah Senior High School
Peoria, Illinois
Graduated June, 1987
Honors and Activities: school newspaper
assistant editor and official photographer,
drama club, swimming team captain

References

Mr. Ric Bessford
Bassi Agency
1647 West Main Street
Peoria, IL 61604

Mr. Paul Hennessy
Casey, Jones and Powell, Inc.
141 West Pierce Street
Chicago, IL 60611

Let us assume that you have a clear track, that the agency you are working for is successful and growing, and that you have the necessary ability. In that case, it would not be remarkable for your steps up the ladder to proceed at a fairly fast pace, possibly on the following schedule:

- $1\frac{1}{2}$ years training in media
- 2 years as an assistant account executive
- 5 years as account executive and senior account executive
- 2 to 3 years as account manager, becoming a vice-president
- 3 to 5 years as management supervisor, becoming either executive vice-president or senior vice-president, depending on the agency's structure
- agency president

At some point during your advancement, you will become a member of the agency's board of directors and perhaps a stockholder. And as you progress, you will have opportunities to acquire increasing amounts of stock in the agency. Exactly the same kind of progression takes place on the creative side of the business; it also can happen in media or research.

It used to be a rarity for a large and prestigious agency to have a president (or chief executive officer) who was not well into his or her forties; however, this is no longer the case, especially in advertising. So, if you are especially dynamic and talented, you can make it to the top in a relatively short time.

Women and Minorities

Is all this opportunity for men only? By no means. One of the biggest and most successful agencies in the country, Wells, Rich, Greene, Inc., was started by a woman, Mary Wells Lawrence, and she was its only chief executive officer for many years. More and more women are sitting on agency boards of directors and holding top positions as advertising directors in large corporations. The trend in this direction is strong but men still outnumber women in most important posts. There is a high proportion of women in lower-level jobs. However, there are still many different types of opportunities for women at all levels. An ambitious and talented woman can confidently expect to get ahead in the advertising business as quickly and as far as her abilities will take her.

It should be acknowledged, however, that at this point, most of the very successful women have risen to the top from early experience in the media, research, or creative sides of business. So far, except for fields like fashion, cosmetics, food, and other areas of traditional feminine interest, not many women have held high-level jobs in account management. It is not altogether clear why this should be, but as of this writing, it is a fact. It will change as time goes on, if enough capable women are interested in advertising careers.

If you are a member of a minority group and have the necessary talent, advertising offers real opportunities for you. Every sizable company and agency is eager to add people of varied ethnic backgrounds to their staff. In most advertising centers they are in great demand and also in very short supply. And as growing numbers of agencies continue to recognize the rewards of marketing to ethnic groups as special markets, these opportunities will increase.

There are also African-American or Spanish-speaking advertising agencies, and these are concentrated mostly in the very largest cities. Generally, they specialize in advertising to the African-American or Spanish-speaking communities and solicit business to reach these sectors only. These agencies have grown tremendously in recent years and offer many opportunities.

FREELANCING OR STARTING YOUR OWN AGENCY

Nearly everyone gets started in advertising working for someone else, whether that someone is an advertising agency, an in-house advertising staff for an advertiser, or a firm specializing in some aspect of advertising. Before you consider freelancing—that is, selling your creative or marketing skills as an individual to various advertisers and advertising agencies—or starting an agency of your own, you need to gain experience and enough skill to make yourself marketable to prospective clients.

Freelancing provides a good first step in self-employment, especially for people in the creative side of advertising. As a freelance artist or copywriter, you will probably work on a project-by-project basis for either the advertising agency or for the advertiser placing the ad. You will very likely do many of the same things that you would do if you were working for the client or agency.

Successful freelancing hinges on understanding and executing with speed whatever is needed. There is no employer to train you. If you want to freelance, you must know your business. Of course, unlike a steady job with an advertiser, you will have to go out and find the work yourself. You cannot simply wait until someone brings it to you. The skill with which you make and expand your job contacts can be a deciding factor in how successful you are at freelancing. Join a professional organization and keep track of former colleagues as they may know about work.

Freelancing has many pluses. If you are good and develop a reputation, you have the potential to earn more than an employee. Of course, unlike a steady job you can't always count on a paycheck coming once or twice a month. Sometimes there will be no work and sometimes people will take a long time to pay, so you must have financial reserves to carry you through slow times. You also have the satisfaction and flexibility of being your own boss. Of course, you may find yourself working harder than ever. This will undoubtedly be true during the first years when you are trying to establish yourself. Since you will probably have to pay the media, suppliers, and operating expenses before you have received payment from your clients, it is essential that you have enough cash reserves (at least six months of estimated operating expenses is recommended) to set up shop. And since some clients will take up to four or five months to pay their bills, this estimate may be conservative. Do not forget that you have to eat and pay your staff as well. So by all means, take the plunge, if you have the experience and think the time is right. But before you jump, test the water.

Once an agency has been in business for a while, its owners may want to become members of the American Association of Advertising Agencies (AAAA). Gaining membership in this organization is a good bit harder than getting started in the business. The agency must be able to demonstrate its financial stability, must be prepared to adhere to the AAAA's code of practice, must be nominated by another agency, must be approved by other members who know it, and must be able to secure references from a number of media with which it has done business. In short, it must be recognized as responsible, established, and professional.

If you decide that starting your own agency would be a great idea, be sure that you consult a lawyer, get the support of a banker, and establish satisfactory credit arrangements with the media that your clients are going to use. It is too important and risky a step to take without careful planning.

THE ROLE OF PUBLIC RELATIONS
AND PUBLICITY SPECIALISTS

Public relations and publicity are closely related to advertising. Both try to create good impressions of a product, idea, or service to the public. Some agencies even have their own public relations departments. Despite their names, however, these groups almost always function as publicity departments. True public relations (PR) is just what the term implies—the art of relating the affairs of an organization and of communicating a favorable impression of the firm. The art of having good public relations was once described as being 95 percent what you do and 5 percent what you say. As a result, public relations counselors and consultants advise their clients on their actions as well as on their words. In doing so, they deal with the very top people in the company or companies they serve. Thus, they are required to have a highly developed sense of what people outside the organization are thinking and how they are likely to react to a given step the company intends to take. Public relations professionals need to be mature and have extremely perceptive judgment of what will be of interest to the public. Like advertising, public relations professionals must combine an ability to sell their ideas to the public with the skill of communicating well in writing.

The principal job of many public relations departments is to write press releases on matters concerning the company, from the company president's position on a major lawsuit to perhaps the appointment of a new director of the mailroom. Press releases are created on new products, major changes in corporate policy, and corporate positions on various issues. Writing simple press releases is often one of the first jobs given to a person just starting in the business. Later, as they acquire more writing and public relations skills, professionals may be asked to write speeches for high-ranking corporate officials or articles for publications and reports that represent the organization to stockholders and other groups.

The other principal aspects of public relations are placing the press releases and other public relations stories with the media and arranging for personal appearances for company spokespeople. Just as in advertising, public relations personnel must select those media, whether newspapers, magazines, radio, or television, that will best convey their message to various audiences. However, unlike advertising, identifying the media is not enough. Public relations professionals must convince editors, columnists, talk show producers, and others that the information they want to place is interesting, accurate, and of concern to their audiences. Just as advertising account executives must work with clients to convince them of the desirability of certain advertisements, the public relations professional must work with clients to convince them how to present material and at the same time work with outside media to convince them to use this material in a manner favorable to the client.

As you can see, public relations is a demanding field and one that uses many of the same skills and makes many of the same contacts with clients and media as advertising does.

CHAPTER 8

MORE OPPORTUNITIES IN ADVERTISING

In addition to the jobs available in the country's 6,000 advertising agencies, many other employment opportunities exist for those interested in the advertising business. We have already touched briefly on the role of advertising departments in manufacturing companies, retailers, and other marketers of goods and services. Jobs relating to advertising also can be found with media, printers, art studios, and others who work closely with advertising agencies and clients, and with public relations and publicity organizations. Each can provide a lifetime career with opportunity for advancement, security, and personal satisfaction.

PUBLIC RELATIONS AND PUBLICITY OPPORTUNITIES

Few advertising agencies engage in all of the public relations functions found in full-time PR agencies. Publicity and public relations differ from advertising in various ways. As we mentioned earlier, advertising is written and placed exactly as the advertiser wants, since the client pays for it. Publicity, on the other hand, and its use and final wording are determined entirely by the editorial staffs of the media to which it is submitted. In short, the advertiser controls the advertisement, and the media controls publicity.

Publicity obviously involves some risks not present in advertising. The media may completely change a press release by the way in which it is rewritten. On the other hand, publicity does provide free exposure for the product or service. And of great importance, skillfully prepared publicity material, appearing as editorial matter, adds credibility to the product or service.

Publicity can take many forms and has many uses. The following is only a sampling of the most common activities:

- *New products or services.* In areas in which there is genuine public interest, many news and picture releases are accepted almost verbatim by the media. Examples of general interest would be the introduction of a new television set or a new kind of car. The real challenge comes in getting coverage for items of intrinsically low public interest value, such as tires, paint, or floor wax.

- *Product demonstrations.* Many household and personal use products lend themselves to demonstration on TV daytime talk shows, and publicity, like the opening of an exciting new film from Hollywood, may find its way onto national telecast evening news programs.

- *Case histories.* Some products and their applications lend themselves to more comprehensive coverage. These might include the development of the personal home computer or the progress being made in the cure of a fatal disease.
- *Newsworthy promotional devices.* Some kinds of merchandise are of sufficient interest to the public to make it easy to put together special events and thereby become real news. Advance fashion news through the showing of a top designer's latest creations provides a good example of what could be developed into a major public relations event.
- *Use of prominent personalities.* Some items can be publicized by the endorsement of public figures whose daily activities are news in themselves. They generally expect an endorsement fee, of course. The professional race car driver's endorsement of STP may be shown on the hat he wears as he is interviewed on TV after crossing the finish line or a golfer with the name "Titleist" prominently displayed on his golf bag.
- *Contrived events.* These promotions are usually designed to capture the audience at sports contests or other activities at which there are large crowds. The list of such possibilities is far too long to spell out here, but they can include "Budweiser Beer Night" at a baseball game, "Marlboro" awards at a rodeo, and the Goodyear blimp.
- *Day-to-day activities.* Publicity involves considerable work that is not necessarily very glamorous. These include announcements of the election or promotion of

an executive, the opening or closing of plants or other facilities, the appointment of an employee to the chairmanship of some community enterprise, and other similar activities.

- *Personal publicity.* This assignment is designed to enhance the reputation and fame of a business executive or other highly placed person. It can involve ghostwriting speeches and articles and arranging for the executive or personality to appear as a guest on television and radio talk shows or at meetings of their peers.
- *Financial publicity or PR.* This is highly specialized work dealing with the release of financial news and reports, including glorifying the company to stockholders. This writing job sounds simple; however, it is not always easy to favorably influence the financial community and not antagonize labor unions and federal regulatory bodies.
- *PR advertising.* Advertising is often used as a means of telling the public about a company's activities, problems, policies, and goals. In time of war, or during periods of shortages or in response to public criticism, the volume of PR (or corporate) advertising always increases sharply.

Topflight publicity people need a highly developed promotional flair, advanced writing skills, keen perception of what is and what is not newsworthy, and as many useful connections with the media as they can develop. In some fields, a depth of technical knowledge also is required.

COMPANY ADVERTISING DEPARTMENTS

Throughout this book we have concentrated primarily on employment opportunities in advertising agencies.

Company advertising departments, on the other hand, offer an equally attractive opportunity for lifetime careers in advertising. These departments set advertising policy for their companies, establish advertising goals, make sure the advertising prepared by their agencies fits company sales and marketing objectives, and keep agencies up-to-date on what the company's management personnel are thinking and doing. Advertising departments are chief sources for all the information agencies need—either directly or through responsible people in other company functions.

The advertising department is held accountable for the agency's performance and for the quality and effectiveness of the advertising and the advertising plan prepared by the agency. It usually has the power to approve or disapprove the agency's recommendations. It always can reject an advertising recommendation proposed by the agency. However, in some cases, final approval must come from a higher level of management. In some companies, the advertising department can hire and fire agencies; in others, it can only recommend such action to top management. It is fair to say that the more important the advertising is to the sale of the company's product, the more top management makes the final decision.

In companies that have more than one agency working for them, the advertising department is responsible for directing and coordinating the work of the different agencies. The department must make sure that advertising for each product is on target and consistent with company goals and policies. Additionally, corporate media contracts must be prepared and maintained to ensure that no one issue of a magazine is scheduled to carry too many advertisements for the company's products while the next issue, for example, carries none. The advertising department also must make sure that the company gets the lowest possible rate for its advertising. Most media have frequency rates that reduce the unit cost when six, twelve, or more advertisements are bought by one advertiser.

The advertising department also handles the budget, which includes expenditures for time and space, production, and all the internal costs of running the department—payroll, rent, heat, lights—everything that is properly chargeable to this separate function.

Many such departments create and produce direct mail material and brochures, catalogs, product labels and packaging, and point-of-sale material, although this work sometimes is done by an outside agency. But wherever these activities occur, it is the function of the advertising department to keep all the advertising and promotional matter in harmony, directed toward the same goals, and consistent in tone and approach.

In small companies, the advertising department generally is run by the advertising manager, with the help of one or two assistants. In big corporations, the department is likely to be headed by an advertising vice president or a director of advertising who presides over separate advertising units, each under the direction of an advertising manager. In some cases, the department has its own research unit; in others, there is a separate research department that assists advertising.

Advertising departments are staffed in very much the same way as agencies. They employ the same kinds of people, with the same qualifications, doing the same work. The big difference is that the advertising department can make final decisions and commit the company's funds to do a job.

The advertising manager or director needs the same skills as the account manager or account executive. Obviously, the other specialists—writers, designers, researchers, or media people—must have exactly the same talents and abilities as their agency counterparts.

One essential difference between working for an agency and working in a company advertising department is that you can hope to become the chief executive of your agency some day, but it is less likely for someone out of the advertising department to get to be the president of the company. That is a significant distinction.

On the other hand, salaries for very high corporate advertising positions can be significantly higher than comparable jobs in agencies. Some companies have house agencies whose structures, jobs, functions, and specialties are similar to those of any independent advertising agency. The only differences are that they work for just one client, are housed within the physical structure of the company, and are paid by the corporation that controls them. Because the people who work in such agencies are paid salaries like other company employees, they are less concerned with profit and loss than are the employees of independently owned agencies.

MEDIA ADVERTISING OPPORTUNITIES

Another profession closely related to all aspects of the advertising business is working for the advertising departments of media companies on their advertising sales staffs. The advertising departments of media firms must function just like the advertising departments of other companies.

There is no essential difference between the activities of the advertising departments in media firms and those of advertisers. Media use direct mail more heavily than most advertisers because the ad agencies and advertisers whom they wish to influence are easy to identify and relatively few in number. This makes direct mail ideal for their purposes.

The function of the advertising sales department is to sell space in their publications or time on their stations or networks to agencies and advertisers. As a result, they call on advertisers and their agencies and consequently find themselves totally immersed in the day-to-day world of advertising dealing directly with company ad executives and calling upon agency media and account people. This selling is done on a one-on-one personal basis and through presentations to groups of agency and client people.

The person in charge of the advertising sales department is generally either the advertising sales manager or the advertising sales director. This individual is usually an excellent salesperson who has risen to the top due to sales performance, sales managerial skills, the ability to train and motivate others, and good contacts. Advertising sales departments are likely to have a research person or department. It is important because much media selling is based on numerical claims and audience activity. The latter can include such details as how many men, women, children, of what ages, and of what income ranges are reached by the media; and the costs an advertiser pays to reach a thousand of such readers or viewers. This information is compared to competitive media. Researchers working in media firms need the same qualifications and abilities as those who work for agencies or advertisers. The big difference in their jobs, however, is that their findings help sell the media for which they work, while agency researchers provide analytical tools for planning advertising campaigns for their clients.

Although the skills required of creative and research people in media are similar to those of their counterparts in advertising agencies, the jobs of advertising sales representatives require very specialized personal attributes and talents. Sales representatives should be personable, highly articulate, persuasive, and extremely knowledgeable about their media and competitors, particularly as they relate to the needs and sales objectives of the prospect. What this means is that, like a good agency account person, a top-flight media sales representative should devote a great deal of time and effort in studying and understanding the prospect's business—the problems, opportunities, and competition. The surest way to be an unsuccessful advertising sales representative is to approach an advertiser or agency with a briefcase full of solutions to problems that do not exist. In any field of advertising, it is vitally important to approach each prospect or assignment as fully armed with specific information and background as is humanly possible. Always be well prepared. It will lead to success and save a lot of embarrassment and grief.

In addition to advertising sales opportunities with media firms, there are a number of independent advertising sales firms. They offer excellent careers for people who enjoy both sales and advertising. Generally they specialize in one area of the media, such as newspapers or radio and TV or magazines. The larger firms offer on-the-job training and good supervision and guidance. Working for such firms offers diversification since you generally work on more than one magazine or newspaper and you become knowledgeable about many markets.

Because people working in media sales are so close to advertisers and advertising agencies, they usually develop good contacts within these organizations. And, since many of the skills needed in the two professions are similar, working in advertising sales can be either a valuable first step in an advertising career or a lifetime profession. Developing skills in advertising sales work can lead to positions such as advertising director of a magazine, radio station, or broadcast network. In the print field, it can lead to top-level positions such as publisher of a large magazine. Advertising sales is the basis for most media income, and being successful in this area can lead to excellent personal and financial rewards.

RECOMMENDED READING

CAREER GUIDANCE

Carter, Robert, and S. William Pattis. *Opportunities in Publishing Careers.* Lincolnwood, IL: VGM Career Horizons, 1995.

Field, Shelly. *Career Opportunities in Advertising and Public Relations.* New York: Facts on File, 1990.

Ganim, Barbara. *How to Approach an Advertising Agency & Walk Away with the Job You Want.* Lincolnwood, IL: NTC Publishing Group, 1993.

Gordon, Barbra. *Opportunities in Commercial Art and Graphic Design Careers.* Lincolnwood, IL: VGM Career Horizons, 1992.

National Association of Broadcasters. *Careers in Television.* Washington, DC.

Noronha, Shonan. *Careers in Communications.* Lincolnwood, IL: VGM Career Horizons, 1993.

Paetro, Maxine. *How to Put Your Book Together and Get a Job in Advertising.* Chicago: Copy Workshop, 1990.

Pattis, S. William. *Careers in Advertising.* Lincolnwood, IL: VGM Career Horizons, 1990.

Resumes for Advertising Careers. Lincolnwood, IL: VGM
Career Horizons, 1993.
Rotman, Morris. *Opportunities in Public Relations Careers.*
Lincolnwood, IL: VGM Career Horizons, 1995.
Steinberg, Margery. *Opportunities in Marketing Careers.*
Lincolnwood, IL: VGM Career Horizons, 1993.
White, Roderick. *Advertising: What It Is and How To Do It.*
New York: McGraw-Hill Book Company, 1993.

THEORY AND PRACTICE

Barry, Ann Marie. *The Advertising Portfolio.* Lincolnwood, IL:
NTC Business Books, 1990.
Book, Albert C. and Dennis Schick. *Fundamentals of Copy
and Layout.* Lincolnwood, IL: NTC Business Books, 1990.
Burton, Philip Ward and Scott C. Purvis. *Which Ad Pulled
Best?: 50 Case Histories on How To Write and Design Ads
That Work.* 7th ed. Lincolnwood, IL: NTC Business Books,
1992.
Dennison, Dell and Linda Tobey. *The Advertising Handbook:
Make a Big Impact with a Small Business Budget.*
Vancouver: International Self-Counsel Press, 1991.
Edwards, Paul, Sarah Edwards, and Laura Clampitt Douglas.
*Getting Business To Come To You: Everything You Need To
Know About Advertising, Public Relations, Direct Mail and
Sales Promotion To Attract All the Business You Can
Handle.* Los Angeles: J.P. Tarcher, 1991.
Gay, Kathlyn. *Caution! This May Be an Advertisement: A Teen
Guide to Advertising.* New York: Franklin Watts, 1992.
Minsky, Laurence, and Emily Thornton Calvo. *How to Succeed
in Advertising When All You Have is Talent.* Lincolnwood,
IL: NTC Business Books, 1994.

Norins, Hanley. *The Young & Rubicam Traveling Creative Workshop.* Englewood Cliffs, NJ: Prentice Hall, 1990.

Pratkanis, Anthony R. and Elliot Aronson. *Age of Propaganda: The Everyday Use and Abuse of Persuasion.* New York: W.H. Freeman, 1992.

Roman, Kenneth and Jane Maas. *The New How To Advertise.* 1st ed. New York: St. Martin's Press, 1992.

Schultz, Don E., Dennis G. Martin, and William P. Brown. *Strategic Advertising Campaigns.* 3d ed. Lincolnwood, IL: NTC Business Books, 1994.

Sroge, Maxwell. *How to Create Successful Catalogs.* Lincolnwood, IL: NTC Business Books, 1995.

Stone, Bob. *Direct Marketing Success Stories.* Lincolnwood, IL: NTC Business Books, 1995.

Stone, Bob. *Successful Direct Marketing Methods.* Lincolnwood, IL: NTC Business Books, 1988.

White, Roderick. *Advertising: What It Is and How To Do It.* New York: McGraw-Hill Book Company, 1993.

DIRECTORIES

Advertising Options Plus: SRDS Directory of Out-of-Home Media
3004 Glenview Road
Wilmette, IL 60091

Broadcasting Cable Yearbook
R.R. Bowker
121 Chanlon Road
New Providence, NJ 07974

Newspaper Rate and Data
3004 Glenview Road
Wilmette, IL 60091

Standard Directory of Advertisers
National Register Publishing Company
121 Chanlon Road
New Providence, NJ 07974

Standard Directory of Advertising Agencies
National Register Publishing Company
121 Chanlon Road
New Providence, NJ 07974

Standard Rate and Data Service
3004 Glenview Road
Wilmette, IL 60091

Working Press of the Nation
Reed Reference Publishing
121 Chanlon Road
New Providence, NJ 07974

PERIODICALS

Ad Business Report, New York, NY.

Advertising Age, Crain Communications, Chicago, IL.

Adweek, Adweek Inc., New York, NY.

American Demographics, Ithica, New York, NY.

Brandweek, Adweek Inc., New York, NY.

Briefings, Advertising Specialty Institute, Langhorne, PA.

Business Marketing, Crain Communications, Chicago, IL.

Creative, Magazines/Creative Inc., New York, NY.

Direct, Cowles Media Group, Stamford, CT.

Folio, Cowles Media Group, Stamford, CT.

Inside Media, Cowles Media Group, Stamford, CT.

Journal of Advertising Research, Advertising Research Foundation, New York, NY.

Journal of Marketing, American Marketing Association, Chicago, IL.

Marketing and Media Decisions, Act III Publishing, New York, NY.

Marketing News, American Marketing Association, Chicago, IL.

PR Reporter, PR Publications Company Inc., Exeter, NH.

Public Relations Journal, Public Relations Society of America, New York, NY.

Quarterly Report: Association of National Advertisers, Advertising/Communications Times, Philadelphia, PA.

Sales and Marketing Management, Bill Communications, New York, NY.

COLLEGE ADVERTISING PROGRAMS

A selected list of colleges offering programs in advertising is presented below. Every effort has been made to make this a comprehensive list, but as changes can occur rapidly, you should also check with local and state schools and with the American Advertising Federation for any additional choices at the time you wish to choose a school.

In addition to colleges offering advertising programs, many other schools have courses in marketing, journalism, design, and other advertising-related courses that you also will want to investigate.

Alabama

University of Alabama
University 35486

Arizona

Northern Arizona University
Flagstaff 86001

Arkansas

University of Arkansas/Little Rock
Little Rock 72204

California

Chapman University
Orange 92666

Pepperdine University
Malibu 90265

San Jose State University
San Jose 95192

University of San Francisco
San Francisco 94117

Colorado

University of Colorado
Boulder 80309

Connecticut

University of Bridgeport
Bridgeport 06602

Florida

University of Florida
Gainesville 32611

Georgia

University of Georgia
Athens 30602

Illinois

Bradley University
Peoria 61625

Columbia College
Chicago 60605

Northwestern University
Evanston 60201

Southern Illinois University
Carbondale 62901

University of Illinois
Urbana 61801

Indiana

Ball State University
Muncie 47306

Purdue University
West Lafayette 47907

Iowa

Drake University
Des Moines 50311

Kentucky

Murray State University
Murray 42071

University of Kentucky
Lexington 40506

Western Kentucky University
Bowling Green 42101

Louisiana

Louisiana State University
Baton Rouge 70803

Maryland

University of Baltimore
Baltimore 21228

Massachusetts

Boston University
Boston 02215

Simmons College
Boston 02115

Michigan

Ferris State College
Big Rapids 49307

Michigan State University
East Lansing 48824

Western Michigan University
Kalamazoo 49001

Minnesota

University of Minnesota
Minneapolis 55455

University of St. Thomas
St. Paul 55105

Winona State University
Winona 55987

Mississippi

University of Southern Mississippi
Hattiesburg 39401

Nebraska

University of Nebraska
Lincoln 68588

New Hampshire

Franklin Pierce College
Rindge 03461

New Jersey

Thomas Edison State College
Trenton 08608

New York

College of New Rochelle
New Rochelle 10801

New York Institute of Technology
Old Westbury 11568

Syracuse University
Syracuse 13210

North Carolina

Campbell University
Buies Creek 27506

North Dakota

University of North Dakota
Grand Forks 58202

Ohio

Columbus College of Art and Design
Columbus 43215

Kent State University
Kent 44242

Marietta College
Marietta 45750

Ohio University
Athens 47501

Youngstown State University
Youngstown 44555

Oklahoma

University of Oklahoma
Norman 73019

Pennsylvania

Cedar Crest College
Allentown 18104

Marywood College
Scranton 18509

Pennsylvania State University
University Park 16802

South Carolina

University of South Carolina
Columbia 29208

South Dakota

South Dakota State University
Brookings 57007

Tennessee

Middle Tennessee State University
Murphreesboro 37132

University of Tennessee
Knoxville 37919

Texas

Abilene Christian University
Abilene 79699

Southern Methodist University
Dallas 75275

Texas Tech University
Lubbock 79409

University of Texas at Austin
Austin 78712

Utah

Weber State University
Ogden 84408

Virginia

Liberty University
Lynchberg 24506

Wisconsin

Marquette University
Milwaukee 53233

APPENDIX C

NATIONAL GROUPS
AND ASSOCIATIONS

The Advertising Council
261 Madison Avenue/11th Floor
New York, NY 10016

Advertising Research Foundation
601 Lexington Avenue
New York, NY 10022

Advertising Women of New York
153 East 57th Street
New York, NY 10022

American Advertising Federation
1400 K Street NW
Suite 1000
Washington, DC 20005

American Association of Advertising Agencies
666 Third Avenue
New York, NY 10017

American Institute of Graphic Arts
164 Fifth Avenue
New York, NY 10010

American Marketing Association
  250 South Wacker Drive
  Suite 200
  Chicago, IL 60606

Art Directors Club of New York
  250 Park Avenue South
  New York, NY 10003

Association of National Advertisers
  155 East Forty-fourth Street
  New York, NY 10017

Council of Better Business Bureaus
  4200 Wilson Boulevard/Suite 800
  Arlington, VA 22203

Council of Sales Promotion Agencies
  750 Summer Street
  Stamford, CT 06901

Direct Marketing Association
  11 West Forty-second Street
  New York, NY 10036

International Advertising Association
  342 Madison Avenue
  New York, NY 10017

Magazine Publishers Association
  919 Third Avenue
  New York, NY 10022

National Advertising Review Board
  845 Third Avenue
  New York, NY 10022

National Association of Broadcasters
  1771 N Street NW
  Washington, DC 20036

National Association of Publisher Representatives
320 East Forty-second Street/Suite 402
Suite 1406
New York, NY 10017

Outdoor Advertising Association of America
1850 M Street NW
Suite 1040
Washington, DC 20036

Point of Purchase Advertising Institute
66 North Van Brunt Street
Englewood, NJ 07631

Promotion Marketing Association of America
322 Eighth Avenue
Suite 1201
New York, NY 10001

Public Relations Society of America
33 Irving Place
New York, NY 10003

Radio Advertising Bureau
304 Park Avenue South
New York, NY 10010

Retail Advertising Association
333 North Michigan Avenue
Suite 3000
Chicago, IL 60601

Television Bureau of Advertising
850 Third Avenue
New York, NY 10022

A complete list of titles in our extensive *Opportunities* series

OPPORTUNITIES IN

Accounting
Acting
Advertising
Aerospace
Agriculture
Airline
Animal & Pet Care
Architecture
Automotive Service
Banking
Beauty Culture
Biological Sciences
Biotechnology
Broadcasting
Building Construction Trades
Business Communication
Business Management
Cable Television
CAD/CAM
Carpentry
Chemistry
Child Care
Chiropractic
Civil Engineering
Cleaning Service
Commercial Art & Graphic
  Design
Computer Maintenance
Computer Science
Counseling & Development
Crafts
Culinary
Customer Service
Data Processing
Dental Care
Desktop Publishing
Direct Marketing
Drafting
Electrical Trades
Electronics
Energy
Engineering
Engineering Technology
Environmental
Eye Care
Fashion
Fast Food
Federal Government
Film
Financial

Fire Protection Services
Fitness
Food Services
Foreign Language
Forestry
Gerontology & Aging Services
Health & Medical
High Tech
Home Economics
Homecare Services
Horticulture
Hospital Administration
Hotel & Motel Management
Human Resource
  Management
Information Systems
Installation & Repair
Insurance
Interior Design & Decorating
International Business
Journalism
Laser Technology
Law
Law Enforcement &
  Criminal Justice
Library & Information
  Science
Machine Trades
Marine & Maritime
Marketing
Masonry
Medical Imaging
Medical Technology
Metalworking
Military
Modeling
Music
Nonprofit Organizations
Nursing
Nutrition
Occupational Therapy
Office Occupations
Paralegal
Paramedical
Part-time & Summer Jobs
Performing Arts
Petroleum
Pharmacy
Photography
Physical Therapy
Physician

Physician Assistant
Plastics
Plumbing & Pipe Fitting
Postal Service
Printing
Property Management
Psychology
Public Health
Public Relations
Publishing
Purchasing
Real Estate
Recreation & Leisure
Refrigeration & Air
  Conditioning
Religious Service
Restaurant
Retailing
Robotics
Sales
Secretarial
Social Science
Social Work
Special Education
Speech-Language Patholog
Sports & Athletics
Sports Medicine
State & Local Government
Teaching
Teaching English to Speake
  of Other Languages
Technical Writing &
  Communications
Telecommunications
Telemarketing
Television & Video
Theatrical Design &
  Production
Tool & Die
Transportation
Travel
Trucking
Veterinary Medicine
Visual Arts
Vocational & Technical
Warehousing
Waste Management
Welding
Word Processing
Writing
Your Own Service Busir

VGM Career Horizons
a division of *NTC Publishing Group*
4255 West Touhy Avenue
Lincolnwood, Illinois 60646–1975